I USED TO GET LONELY, BUT NOT ANYMORE..

T0387722

THE COMPLETE PEANUTS
by Charles M. Schulz

Fantagraphics Books, Inc.

Editor: Gary Groth

Designer: Kayla E.

Production, assembly, and restoration: Paul Baresh

Archival and production assistance: Marcie Lee, Daniel Johnson, Lucy Kiester, and Caroline Sibila

Associate Publisher: Eric Reynolds

Publisher: Gary Groth

Special thanks to Jean Schulz, without whom this project would not have come to fruition.

Thanks to Timothy Chow, and to Charles M. Schulz Creative Associates, especially Paige Braddock and Kim Towner.

Fantagraphics Books, Inc.,
7563 Lake City Way NE,
Seattle, WA 98115, USA

www.peanuts.com

www.fantagraphics.com

ISBN: 979-8-8750-0010-2

Library of Congress Control Number: 2024933680

First softcover printing: 2024

Printed in China

PEANUTS

The COMPLETE PEANUTS by CHARLES M. SCHULZ 1993–1994

HERE, BOY!
"BOY"?

Introduction by

JAKE TAPPER

WHEN I WAS A LITTLE BOY, MY MOTHER WORRIED about how much I loved *Peanuts*. Specifically, she fretted that I identified too closely with Charlie Brown.

In retrospect, my *Peanuts* preoccupation was mostly motivated by a love of cartooning and my appreciation for Charles "Sparky" Schulz's sense of humor and graphic skill. But I don't want to dismiss my mother's concerns, because they weren't without merit.

While other cartoon characters' "humor" was rooted in gluttony (Garfield, Hagar the Horrible) or mischief (Dennis the Menace), Charlie Brown's defining characteristic has been for decades his insecurity.

And that, yes, I could relate to. I suspect most of us can, even though insecurity is something we all so rarely discuss.

It's hardly an original observation to suggest that *Peanuts* is so popular not because Charlie Brown is a loser whom we all deride, but rather because he's someone to whom we can all relate. Whose life has not included an unattainable love like the little red-haired girl? Who does not have a kite-eating tree lurking, existentially? Who does not return, on blind faith, time after time, to try to kick that football?

But the thing about Charlie Brown: he's not a loser.

Charlie Brown, when all is said and done, is a winner. Yes, he has struggles and insecurities, disappointments and dark voices in the middle of the night, as do we all. And yes, he's a C-student (not unlike some Presidents.) But Charlie Brown has a good life and a loving family. He has friends. A sister who adores him. A fun dog who depends upon him. He's the manager of his baseball team. And while he might be either blissfully unaware or not interested, there are plenty of girls who seem to dig him.

Charles Schulz himself was a winner, though how much he let himself enjoy his tremendous bounty is debatable. Interviews with him are a mix of confidence and doubts. The man revealed is both assured of his achievements in the popular culture, while also longing for Olympian heights he cannot reach as well as his own metaphorical "Rosebud" sleds from his past.

Schulz's farewell to his mother, on her cancer death bed in 1943, was a heartbreak that never healed. Then just 20, a soldier shipping to Europe but home with a day pass from Fort Snelling, Sparky visited his mom and before he left heard her say "Goodbye, Sparky. We'll probably never see each other again." He would later suggest that he never fully recovered from that moment.

For all the talk of his loneliness and anxiety, Schulz was not without ego; he fully understood what he had accomplished. Some have portrayed this as a contradiction, but it isn't. The ghosts that haunt us from our past — bullies, a parent's sudden and early death, rejections romantic and professional — do not vanish upon success. Making the *Forbes* list did not bring Schulz's mother back to life. High ratings for his TV specials did not make Donna Mae Johnson, the actual little red-haired girl, accept his marriage proposal.

"I can think of no more emotionally damaging loss than to be turned down by someone whom you love very much," Schulz told one biographer. "A person who not only turns you down, but almost immediately will marry the victor. What a bitter blow that is."

Of course one has to wonder how much Schulz nurtured that red-haired loss for the sake of his art. After all, as Schulz once quipped to the actual Shermy, "I got my money's worth out of that relationship."

It is indeed this laying bare the disappointments of life upon the page that makes *Peanuts* so resonant. We tend not to discuss our feelings of inadequacy, our fears of others' distaste for us. To do so, we are taught, is weak. And so the charade continues.

And, though I confess that I'm happy that my son identifies more with Snoopy than with his owner, this is why the notion that Charlie Brown is indeed a winner is so important for *Peanuts* fans. Because he, and Sparky, are us.

"The poetry of these children is born from the fact that we find in them all the problems, all the sufferings of the adults, who remain offstage," Umberto Eco wrote in his introduction to the first *Peanuts* collection in Italian.

The very first cartoon in this volume occurs on New Year's Day. Peppermint Patty is calling Charlie Brown to ask if he loves her. His response is hardly satisfying, and a reminder that Charlie Brown is not the only one who suffers unrequited love: when one factors in goals such as defeating the Red Baron, returning to the happy days of the Daisy Hill Puppy Farm or witnessing an appearance by the Great Pumpkin, virtually all the characters pine for something or someone out of reach. Sally loves Linus, Lucy

loves Schroeder, Peppermint Patty and Marcie compete for Charlie Brown's affection. Within these pages, we are also introduced to another young girl who takes a fancy to our hero, one who claims to be Roy Hobbs' great-granddaughter — despite the continued reminders to the girl that Malamud's *The Natural* was a work of fiction.

A few of the strips in this volume contain zeitgeist-y references that may now date them — Peppermint Patty confusing Snow White with Vanna White, Snoopy as Joe Grunge, a discussion of Snoopy facing then-Sen. Joe Biden, chair of the Judiciary Committee in 1993. But for the most part they land in the timeless suburb that enables *Peanuts* to continue in syndication today. Most of the cultural references are similarly timeless: Mickey Mouse, Alice in Wonderland, and Willy Loman.

Leo Tolstoy continues to be a frequent *Peanuts* touchstone; Schulz thought *War and Peace* the greatest novel ever written, and he could relate to the author's demons. "He sure went through a lot of turmoil," Schulz told *The Comics Journal* in 1997. "And he also had what Scott Fitzgerald talked about once, 'the dark side of the soul,' didn't he...I think perhaps a lot of us have gone through that in different ways. And I don't even know if it can be explained."

In a Summer strip, on page 77, Linus asks Charlie Brown which he would rather do, write *War and Peace* like Tolstoy, or be the first to hit more than 60 home runs in a single season like Roger Maris.

After striking out, Charlie Brown says, "I probably won't write *War and Peace*, either."

Don't be so sure that you didn't, Mr. Schulz. 

HI, CHUCK..JUST CALLING TO WISH YOU A HAPPY NEW YEAR...

1-1-93
DO YOU LOVE ME, CHUCK?

I'M SORRY, BUT YOUR CALL CANNOT GO THROUGH..PLEASE HANG UP, AND DO NOT DIAL AGAIN..
SCHULZ

I'M THINKING MAYBE WHEN I GROW UP, I'LL BE A BEAUTY QUEEN..
1-2-93

DO YOU HAVE TO BE REALLY BEAUTIFUL?
PROBABLY

DO THEY HAVE A SORT OF FAIRLY, KIND OF, YOU KNOW, CUTE QUEEN?
SCHULZ

PEANUTS
by SCHULZ

KING OF THE HILL!

I AM THE KING! I AM THE KING OF THE HILL!
1-3-'93

I AM THE QUEEN! I AM THE QUEEN OF THE HILL!!

I AM THE ATTORNEY! I AM KING OF THE HILL! I HAVE THE DEED OF TRUST!

SCHULZ

"Will you miss me while I'm gone?" he asked.

"Why?" she said. "Where are you going?"

"Don't you remember?" he said. "I'm going on an expedition, and I'll be gone for twenty-five years."
1-4-93

"I'm sorry," she said. "I guess I wasn't listening."
SCHULZ

YES, MA'AM.. I BROUGHT MY DOG TO SCHOOL TODAY.. WELL, SOMETIMES HE GETS LONELY...
1-5-93

NO, MA'AM.. HE WON'T CREATE A DISTURBANCE..
MAYBE..
Z
SCHULZ

MA'AM? MY DOG WANTS TO GO OUT IN THE HALL FOR A DRINK OF WATER..

1-6-93

A LITTLE PROBLEM, MA'AM.. THERE'S A FOUNTAIN OUT THERE, BUT NO WATER DISH.. DO YOU HAVE A WATER DISH?

DOGS ARE WORTH IT, MA'AM..
SCHULZ

A TRUE OR FALSE TEST? YES, MA'AM

DO YOU MIND IF MY DOG TAKES THE TEST, TOO? YOU KNOW, JUST FOR THE FUN OF IT...
1-7-93

IT'LL GIVE HIM SOMETHING TO DO

HOW DO YOU MAKE "T'S" AND "F'S"?
SCHULZ

TRUE..FALSE.. TRUE..FALSE..

TRUE..TRUE.. FALSE..TRUE..

HOW ARE YOU DOING?

1-8-93
SCHULZ
NO PEEKING!

HERE'S MY TEST PAPER, MA'AM..

AND HERE'S MY DOG'S TEST PAPER..

WE NEVER HAD "TRUE OR FALSE" TESTS AT OBEDIENCE SCHOOL

THEY WERE CALLED "SIT OR ELSE"
SCHULZ
1-9-93

PEANUTS
by SCHULZ

NOW WHAT'S HE DOING?

I LOVE TO COME OUT HERE TO MY SNOW COVERED PITCHER'S MOUND AND RELIVE ALL THOSE GOOD MEMORIES..

WHAT GOOD MEMORIES?

THE GAMES WE PLAYED..SOME WE WON..SOME WE LOST..
WE LOST THEM ALL

THERE WERE SOME CLOSE ONES, ALL RIGHT...
LIKE FIFTY-FOUR TO NOTHING..

AND ALL THE PERFECT STRIKES I PITCHED..
AND THE TIME YOU WALKED TWENTY-FOUR HITTERS IN A ROW

1-10

WAP!

THAT'S THE BEST PITCH I THREW ALL YEAR!
SCHULZ

HE DID WHAT?

SHE SAYS YOU GOT THE ONLY PERFECT SCORE ON THE "TRUE OR FALSE" TEST!
1/11

NO, MA'AM, I DON'T KNOW HOW HE DID IT..

WHAT'S TRUE IS TRUE, AND WHAT'S FALSE IS FALSE..
SCHULZ

YES, SIR, MR. PRINCIPAL.. MY TEACHER SENT US HERE TO SEE YOU...

I GUESS MY DOG WAS THE ONLY ONE IN OUR CLASS TO GET A PERFECT SCORE ON THE "TRUE OR FALSE" TEST

TWENTY OUT OF TWENTY..NO, SIR, I HAVE NO IDEA HOW HE DID IT...

WHEN YOU'RE HOT, YOU'RE HOT!
SCHULZ
1-12

NO, SIR.. I DIDN'T HELP HIM.. I DIDN'T KNOW SOME OF THE ANSWERS MYSELF..

1-13
YES, SIR.. HE GOT A PERFECT SCORE... NO, HE DIDN'T CHEAT..
SCHULZ

NO, SIR, WE'RE NOT MAKING FUN OF YOUR SCHOOL..

THEY DON'T BELIEVE YOU COULD GET A PERFECT SCORE ON A "TRUE OR FALSE" TEST, SNOOPY..

SO YOU KNOW WHAT THEY WANT YOU TO DO? THEY WANT YOU TO TAKE AN ESSAY TEST..

THEN I'M GOING HOME..
1-14

DOGS DON'T DO ESSAY TESTS!
SCHULZ

NO, MA'AM..MY DOG DIDN'T COME TO SCHOOL TODAY..

NO, I STILL DON'T KNOW HOW HE GOT A PERFECT SCORE ON THE "TRUE OR FALSE" TEST
1-15

MAYBE IT'LL ALWAYS BE A MYSTERY...

I NEVER CAN REMEMBER..DID THE "T" STAND FOR "TRUE" OR FOR "FALSE"?
SCHULZ

I THINK I'M GETTING SMARTER EVERY DAY..
GOOD FOR YOU

DID YOU KNOW THERE'S NO SCHOOL ON SATURDAYS? I WENT DOWN THERE TODAY, AND ALL THE DOORS WERE LOCKED..
1-16

I FIGURED THAT ONE OUT IN A HURRY!
SCHULZ

AFTER SEVERAL WEEKS HAD GONE BY, SPIKE FINALLY DECIDED THAT HIS NEW BUSINESS VENTURE JUST WASN'T GOING TO MAKE IT..

1-17

SCHULZ

MARTIN LUTHER KING SAID, " I HAVE A DREAM"

BEFORE THAT, WE WOULDN'T BE SITTING HERE..

AND I WOULDN'T BE TRADING YOU A CARROT STICK FOR A FRENCH FRY..
1-18

THAT'S NOT AN EVEN TRADE, FRANKLIN..
SCHULZ

I'VE BEEN WORRIED ABOUT YOU..HOW ARE YOU STANDING THE COLD WEATHER?
1-19

SCHULZ

SCHULZ
TELL THE BUS TO HURRY UP.. I'M FREEZING TO DEATH!
WHERE'S YOUR BROTHER?
I THINK I'M IN HERE SOMEPLACE..
1-20

1-21

"AND THE VOICE OF THE TURTLE IS HEARD IN OUR LAND.."
SCHULZ

THIS IS RIDICULOUS! I'M LIKE A TURTLE.. I CAN'T GET UP!

I COULD LIE HERE ALL WINTER..

MAYBE SOMEONE WILL COME ALONG, AND HELP ME..
1-22

DO YOU MIND IF I PLAY THROUGH?
SCHULZ

WHY ARE YOU LYING HERE ON YOUR BACK LIKE A TURTLE, BIG BROTHER?
1-23

I SLIPPED ON THE ICE, AND NOW I CAN'T GET UP..

I'M GOING TO HAVE TO LIE HERE FOR THE REST OF MY LIFE..

SHOULD I START MOVING MY THINGS INTO YOUR ROOM?
SCHULZ

PEANUTS
by SCHULZ

A LOVE LETTER! I GOT A LOVE LETTER!

HOW CAN IT BE A LOVE LETTER FOR YOU WHEN IT HAS MY NAME ON IT?

IT'S FROM LINUS.. READ IT...

Dear Charlie Brown,
Our family is on a little trip.
We are having a good time.
P.S. Say "Hi" to Sally.

SEE? HE SAID, "SAY 'HI' TO SALLY!"... IF THAT ISN'T A LOVE LETTER, I DON'T KNOW WHAT IS!

1-24
I THINK I'LL PASTE IT IN MY SCRAPBOOK..

MY FIRST LOVE LETTER!
HOW ROMANTIC..
SCHULZ

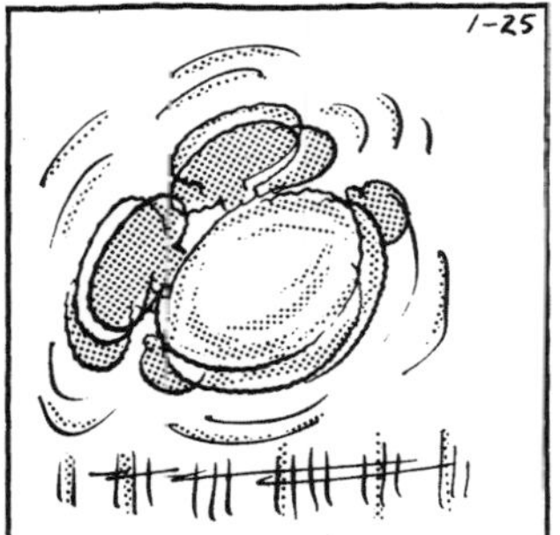
1-25

SCHULZ

SNOOPY! YOU'VE COME TO RESCUE ME! YOU CAN PUSH ME ALL THE WAY HOME..

KEEP PUSHING, BUT BE CAREFUL WHEN WE GET TO THE..

1-26
..CURB!
SCHULZ

HERE'S THE WORLD FAMOUS HOCKEY PLAYER ON HIS WAY TO THE GAME..
1-27

UNDER THE NEW RULES IF YOU START A FIGHT, YOU ARE AUTOMATICALLY EJECTED FROM THE GAME...

SO I MIGHT AS WELL GO HOME NOW..
SCHULZ

Dear Brother Snoopy,
Guess what! It snowed here last night!

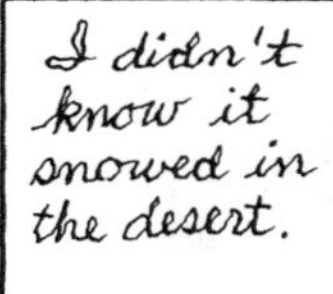
I didn't know it snowed in the desert.

1-28

I guess we learn something new every day, don't we?

WHOP!

Like, I didn't know coyotes could throw.
SCHULZ

LEND ME A PENCIL, WILL YOU, MARCIE?

I DON'T HAVE A PENCIL, MA'AM.. I LENT IT TO THE KID IN FRONT OF ME..
I'M NOT THE "KID" IN FRONT OF YOU!
1-29

LEND ME A COMB, WILL YOU, MARCIE?
DROP DEAD, SIR!
PRINCIPAL'S OFFICE
SCHULZ

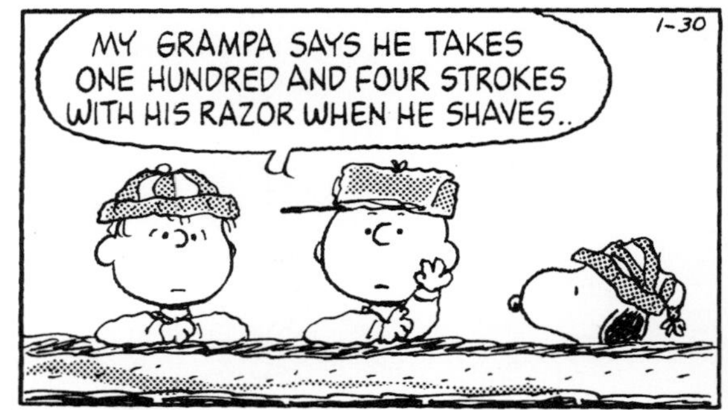
1-30
MY GRAMPA SAYS HE TAKES ONE HUNDRED AND FOUR STROKES WITH HIS RAZOR WHEN HE SHAVES..

HE COUNTED THEM?
GRAMPA IS RETIRED.. HE DOESN'T HAVE MUCH ELSE TO DO..
SCHULZ

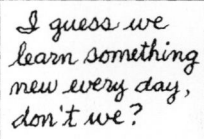

PEANUTS
by SCHULZ

Y'KNOW, I THINK I'VE DISCOVERED SOMETHING ABOUT MYSELF..

BY THE WAY, LOOK OUT FOR THAT TREE DOWN THERE..

AND STEER AWAY FROM THOSE ROCKS AND THAT FENCE..

WHAT IS IT THAT YOU'VE DISCOVERED ABOUT YOURSELF, CHARLIE BROWN?

1-31

I ALWAYS WORRY ABOUT THE WRONG THINGS
SCHULZ

NO, MA'AM.. I WASN'T VOLUNTEERING...

I WAS SIGNALING FOR A FAIR CATCH!

NO, I DIDN'T SEE A POLAR BEAR RUN BY HERE..

DOES HE KNOW YOU'RE CHASING HIM?

YES, THAT'S PROBABLY WHAT HAPPENED..

HE WAS RUNNING SO FAST I DIDN'T SEE HIM..

DIDN'T CATCH THE POLAR BEAR, HUH?

WHAT ARE YOU GOING TO DO NOW?

NO, I DON'T KNOW WHAT A MOOSE TASTES LIKE..

WHAT HAPPENS IF YOU CAN'T SPEAR A POLAR BEAR OR A MOOSE?
2-4

SCHULZ
YOU SPEAR THE WILD CHOCOLATE CHIP COOKIE!

SEE, MARCIE? MY AD IS IN THE PAPER..

"HELP WANTED.. ATTRACTIVE YOUNG LADY CAN'T REMEMBER HISTORY DATES"

"DOESN'T UNDERSTAND FRACTIONS.. CALL PATRICIA REICHARDT AT NUMBER BELOW.."
2-5

WHAT DO YOU THINK, MARCIE?
YOU ARE EXTREMELY WEIRD, SIR
SCHULZ

SOMETIMES I LIE AWAKE AT NIGHT, AND I ASK, "IS IT ALL WORTH IT?"

THEN A VOICE SAYS, "WHO ARE YOU TALKING TO?"

THEN ANOTHER VOICE SAYS, "YOU MEAN, 'TO WHOM ARE YOU TALKING?'"

NO WONDER I LIE AWAKE AT NIGHT!
2-6
SCHULZ

PEANUTS®
by SCHULZ

I HEARD YOU BARKING AGAIN LAST NIGHT..

WHAT WAS GOING ON?

2-7
MY REPORT..

1:00 A.M. Saw a catt on a fence
2:00 A.M. Heard an Owl.
3:15 A.M. Thout I heard a beraguler.

WHAT'S A "BERAGULER"?

IT'S HARD TO WRITE BY THE LIGHT OF THE MOON..
SCHULZ

I HAVE A NEW PHILOSOPHY.. "LIFE IS LIKE A GOLF COURSE"
AND "A SAND TRAP RUNS THROUGH IT"
2-8
SCHULZ

STANDING IN THE RAIN WAITING FOR THE SCHOOL BUS SHOWS A DESIRE FOR AN EDUCATION THAT LEADS TO COLLEGE AND A JOB WITH A BIG SAN FRANCISCO LAW FIRM..
HERE, HIT HIM WITH A LUNCH BOX!
2-9
SCHULZ

YES, MA'AM..MY HEAD SORT OF HURTS...I THINK MAYBE I HAVE THE GOLLYWOPPERS...
2-10

YES, MA'AM..I HAD A FLU SHOT ABOUT A MONTH AGO..
SCHULZ

NO, MA'AM..THE AVERAGE FLU SHOT HAS NO EFFECT ON THE GOLLYWOPPERS..

HOW DID EVERYTHING GO AT SCHOOL TODAY, MARCIE? REMEMBER? I HAD TO GO HOME
2-11

SOMEBODY BROKE INTO THE CUSTODIAN'S CAR, THE DRINKING FOUNTAIN FELL OFF THE WALL, AND THAT STUPID KID IN THE BACK ROW ATE THE LAST PIECE OF CHALK...

RATS! I ALWAYS MISS THE GOOD DAYS!
SCHULZ

SURE, LIFE IN THE DESERT CAN BE LONELY AT TIMES..
2-12

BUT AT LEAST YOU KNOW YOU'RE NOT GOING TO GET HIT IN THE FACE WITH A PIE...

PROBABLY..
SCHULZ

"I DON'T KNOW," SAID THE FARMER.."I'M NOT A COW!"
2-13

HA HAHAHA

ROCKS NEVER LAUGH AT ANYTHING..
SCHULZ

PEANUTS
by SCHULZ
I'VE BEEN THINKING THE SAME THING FOR YEARS..
2-14
KEEP YOUR VALENTINE, KID!
IF SHE DOESN'T LOVE YOU ALREADY, A VALENTINE WON'T HELP!
I'VE BEEN AROUND A LONG TIME, KID.. I KNOW HOW THESE THINGS GO...
TAKE IT FROM ME, KID..THEY'LL BREAK YOUR HEART...KEEP YOUR VALENTINE!
OH, WELL.. WHAT DO I CARE!?
THAT'S A STRANGE NEW MAILBOX DOWN ON THE CORNER..
SCHULZ

THAT LITTLE RED HAIRED GIRL IS AT THE DOOR...

SHE SAYS SHE FORGOT TO GIVE YOU A VALENTINE SO SHE CAME BY TO GIVE IT TO YOU NOW...

APRIL FOOL!!
2-15

..OR FEBRUARY OR MARCH OR WHATEVER
SCHULZ

2-16
DOES YOUR SISTER EVER AGGRAVATE YOU?
HOW MANY HOURS ARE IN THE DAY?
WHAT WAS THE QUESTION?
WHO ARE THEY TALKING ABOUT?
DID SOMEBODY MENTION COOKIES?
SCHULZ

LINUS, DO ME A FAVOR... ASK THAT LITTLE RED-HAIRED GIRL IF SHE EVER GOT THE VALENTINE I SENT HER...

2-17
HEY!

SAY, KID..THE TEACHER WANTS TO KNOW WHY YOU'RE CRAWLING OUT THE DOOR..
SCHULZ

I'LL BE THE SHEPHERD AND YOU BE A SHEEP, OKAY?
2-18

YOU'RE SUPPOSED TO SAY, "BAA!"
SCHULZ

WE SHEPHERDS HAVE A FAVORITE SAYING..

"GOD TEMPERS THE WIND TO THE SHORN LAMB"

WHATEVER THAT MEANS
2-19
SCHULZ

HERE'S THE LONELY SHEPHERD STANDING OUT UNDER THE STARS..

ALL HIS SHEEP HAVE GONE ASTRAY... IT'S SO SAD..

YOU'RE NOT CRYING..
SCHULZ
2-20

PEANUTS
by SCHULZ
I THINK I HEAR A CAN OPENER..

OUCH!

WHOOPS!

2-21
I HOPE YOU APPRECIATE THIS

I ALMOST CUT MYSELF OPENING THE CAN, AND I ALMOST DROPPED IT ALL ON THE FLOOR...

AND I ALMOST FELL DOWN THE STEPS COMING OUT HERE!

AND I APPRECIATE IT MORE THAN ANYTHING IN THE WHOLE WORLD..

ALMOST
SCHULZ

DON'T EVEN THINK IT!
2-22

IF I CAN'T SAY IT, I **HAVE** TO THINK IT..
SCHULZ

IN
OUT
2-23
SCHULZ

WELL, I IMAGINE THE REASON YOU CAN'T THROW A SNOWBALL IS YOU DON'T HAVE ANY HANDS..

OF COURSE, YOU COULD ALWAYS JUST "WING" IT!

HA HA HA HA

2-24
SCHULZ

I'M NOT GOING TO SCHOOL TODAY, MARCIE.. I HAVE A COLD...

SHALL I BRING SOME OF YOUR SCHOOL WORK HOME SO YOU CAN DO IT TONIGHT?
2-25

ARE YOU OUT OF YOUR MIND?

I DON'T UNDERSTAND SICK PEOPLE..
SCHULZ

NO, MA'AM, PATRICIA ISN'T HERE TODAY... SHE HAS A COLD..

NO, MA'AM, SHE DOESN'T WANT ME TO TAKE HER HOMEWORK TO HER..
2-26

ARE YOU OUT OF YOUR MIND?

JUST QUOTING HER, MA'AM..
SCHULZ

2-27
SCHULZ

PEANUTS
by SCHULZ

GOOD NIGHT

Z
Z

Z
+Z
ZZ

ZZZ
Z)ZZZ
Z
Z
Z
Z

ZZZ
×ZZ
ZZZ
ZZZ
ZZZZ

WHAT ARE YOU DOING HERE IN THE KITCHEN, BIG BROTHER?

2-28
CAN'T YOU SLEEP?
IT GOT TOO COMPLICATED..
SCHULZ

HERE'S MY EXCUSE, MA'AM, FOR MISSING SCHOOL LAST WEEK..
3-1

DON'T TRY TO STAND IT UP...IT'S A PRETTY LAME EXCUSE

HAHAHAHA

THANK YOU, MA'AM.. I'M GLAD I'M BACK, TOO..
SCHULZ

3-2

YOU'RE THE ONLY ONE I KNOW WHO CAN LAND WITH BACKSPIN..
SCHULZ

HOW TO FLY A KITE
"THE FLOW OF WIND OVER THE TOP OF THE KITE MOVES FASTER THAN THE AIR BEHIND THE KITE'S LEADING EDGE CREATING A VACUUM WHICH CAUSES LIFT.."
3-3
SCHULZ

FOR "SHOW AND TELL" THIS MORNING I HAVE A TURTLE WHICH I SAVED WHEN IT WAS TRYING TO CROSS THE ROAD..

IT ISN'T ?
3-4

FOR "SHOW AND TELL" THIS MORNING I HAVE A HUBCAP WHICH I SAVED WHEN IT WAS TRYING TO CROSS THE ROAD..
SCHULZ

MY GRAMPA SAYS THAT AFTER ALL THESE YEARS, HE STILL DOESN'T UNDERSTAND LIFE

FOR INSTANCE, LAST WEEK HE BOUGHT A NEW CAR..

3-5
BUT HE GOT THE FLU ANYWAY..
SCHULZ

RATS!

NO MATTER HOW HARD YOU TRY, YOU CAN'T DRIBBLE A TUMBLEWEED!
SCHULZ
3-6

PEANUTS
by SCHULZ

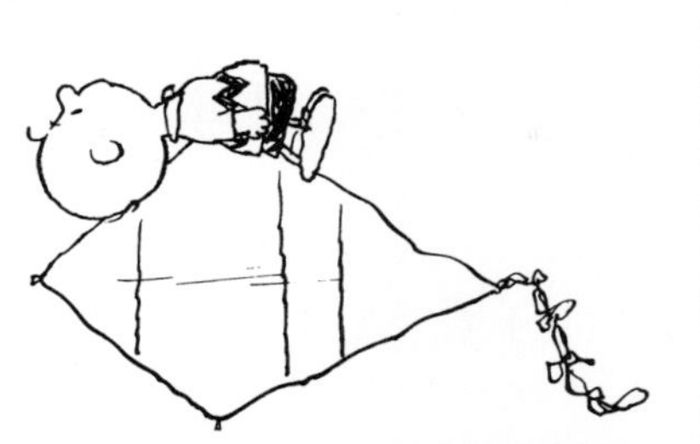

THE DOCTOR
IS IN

PSYCHIATRIC
HELP 5¢
?!
THE DOCTOR
IS IN

3-7

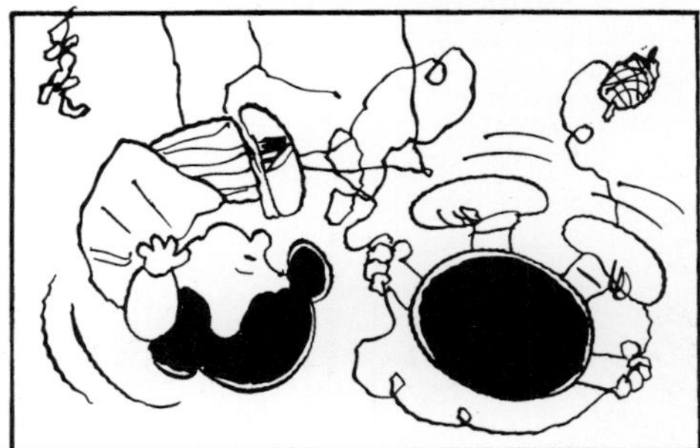

YOU'RE A BLOCKHEAD! FIVE CENTS, PLEASE..
SCHULZ

AH CHOO

BLESS YOU

THIS BUTTER IS PRACTICALLY FROZEN..

NOBODY TOLD ME LIFE WAS GOING TO BE THIS HARD!

I HATE GETTING UP IN THE MORNING.. SCHOOL DRIVES ME CRAZY...

..AND NOW I HAVE TO BUTTER MY TOAST WITH CHUNKY BUTTER!

"CHUNKY" BUTTER?

THIS IS A NICE LIBRARY, MA'AM..

I NEED A COUPLE OF BOOKS...DO YOU HAVE "A TALE OF TWO TOWNS" BY CHARLES WHAT'S-HIS-NAME?

YOU HAVE IT! THIS IS GREAT..

NOW HOW ABOUT "THE BROTHERS SOMETHING OR OTHER"?

IS THE SCHOOL BUS HERE YET?
YOU DON'T SEE IT, DO YOU?

MY, AREN'T WE CRABBY TODAY..
I'M NOT CRABBY.. I FEEL FINE..
3-11

GOOD..MAY I ASK YOU A PERSONAL QUESTION?
SURE, GO RIGHT AHEAD..

IS THE SCHOOL BUS HERE YET?
SCHULZ

YOU'RE ALWAYS SAYING BEETHOVEN WAS SO GREAT...

DID BEETHOVEN EVER SERVE ON A SUB-COMMITTEE? HUH? DID HE?

KLUNK!
3-12

HOW CAN YOU BE CALLED GREAT IF YOU'VE NEVER SERVED ON A SUB-COMMITTEE?
SCHULZ

It was a dark and stormy night.
3-13

HOW CAN YOU BE SO SURE?

If I remember correctly, it was a dark and stormy night.
SCHULZ

PEANUTS
by SCHULZ

OH, NO!

ALL RIGHT! WHO'S BEEN IN MY COMIC BOOKS?!

A STORM IS APPROACHING! EVERYONE TAKE COVER!

YOU'VE BEEN IN MY COMIC BOOKS AGAIN, HAVEN'T YOU?!!
3-14

I TRY TO KEEP THEM IN ORDER, AND NOW YOU'VE MESSED THEM ALL UP! YOU DRIVE ME CRAZY!!

FROM NOW ON, LEAVE THEM ALONE! AND STAY OUT OF MY ROOM!

SCHULZ

THE STORM ABATES... THE SUN COMES OUT.. PEACE REIGNS AGAIN

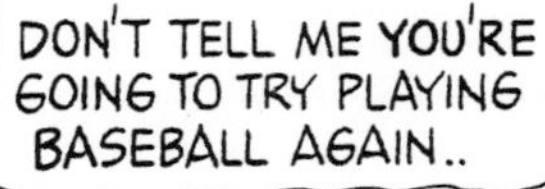
DON'T TELL ME YOU'RE GOING TO TRY PLAYING BASEBALL AGAIN..

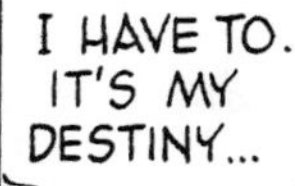
I HAVE TO.. IT'S MY DESTINY...

WHEN SPRING COMES, I'M DRAWN TO THE BALL FIELD! I FORGET EVERYTHING ELSE..
3-15

DON'T FORGET TO FEED THE DOG..
SCHULZ

I CAN'T PLAY TODAY, MANAGER.. I COULDN'T FIND MY GLOVE..

WOULDN'T IT BE FUNNY IF IT TURNED OUT THAT YOUR GLOVE WAS ON YOUR HEAD AND YOUR CAP ON TOP OF YOUR GLOVE?
3-16

I'LL GO HOME AND LOOK AROUND AGAIN..IF I CAN'T FIND IT, JUST START WITHOUT ME..
SCHULZ

NOW, WHEN WE ASK HIM IF YOU CAN PLAY, DON'T LET HIM KNOW YOU'RE SO SHORT

YOU HAVE A FRIEND WHO WANTS TO PLAY ON OUR TEAM?
3-17

WHERE?
SCHULZ

HOW COULD HE PLAY ON OUR TEAM? HE'S TOO SHORT!

SNIF!
3-18

WELL, ASK HIM IF MAYBE HE'D LIKE TO BE OUR BAT BIRD..
SCHULZ

HOW ARE THINGS IN LEFT FIELD, PIGPEN?

I PUT BURNT CORK UNDER MY EYES JUST LIKE THE PROS..

"PAINTING THE LILY," HUH?
PAINTING THE WHAT?

MANAGERS ARE ALWAYS SAYING STRANGE THINGS..
SCHULZ
3-19

ALL RIGHT, EVERYONE OVER HERE FOR THE TEAM PHOTO!
YOU HAVE YOUR CHOICE.. YOU CAN SIT WITH EITHER PIGPEN OR THE DOG...
WHAT KIND OF A CHOICE IS THAT?
I SHOULD THINK IT WOULD BE OBVIOUS
I'LL TAKE TEN 5X7, TWELVE 8X10, AND TWENTY WALLET SIZE..
SCHULZ
3-20

PEANUTS
by SCHULZ
CAPS

WHAT'S GOING ON?

..AND EVERYONE WHO MADE THE TEAM THIS YEAR GETS A NEW CAP!

HERE YOU GO, SCHROEDER.. YOU DESERVE IT..

HERE YOU ARE, PIGPEN.. TRY TO KEEP IT CLEAN...

3-21
THIS IS FOR YOU, SNOOPY, OL' PAL!

HERE YOU GO, LINUS.. A BRAND NEW CAP!

I DON'T KNOW IF I MADE THE TEAM OR NOT..
SCHULZ

I HEARD THE COYOTES HOWLING AGAIN LAST NIGHT, CHARLIE BROWN..

I WONDER IF IT'S AN OMEN THAT WE'RE GOING TO LOSE THE FIRST GAME OF THE SEASON...

THAT'S RIDICULOUS! WE'RE GOING TO WIN! I DON'T BELIEVE IN OMENS..
3-22

BUT THEY SOUNDED SO EERIE..

MAYBE IT WAS AN OMEN THAT WE'RE GOING TO LOSE THE SECOND GAME OF THE SEASON..
SCHULZ

I CAN'T BELIEVE IT..
3-23

OUR BASEBALL SEASON STARTS TODAY, AND WE HAVEN'T LOST YET..

OF COURSE, I HAVEN'T GOTTEN OUT OF BED YET, EITHER..
SCHULZ

I HATE TO WAKE YOU UP, BUT WE HAVE OUR FIRST GAME TODAY..

HERE'S YOUR CAP AND YOUR GLOVE..

EAT A GOOD BREAKFAST..I'M COUNTING ON YOU TO PLAY HARD
3-24

AND DON'T GO BACK TO SLEEP!!
SCHULZ

I FEEL UP FOR THE GAME TODAY! I REALLY THINK WE CAN WIN!

I FEEL GOOD MENTALLY, AND I FEEL GOOD PHYSICALLY.. THIS IS THE MOST CONFIDENT I'VE EVER FELT...
3-25

YOU'VE GOT GRAPE JELLY ON YOUR SHIRT..
SCHULZ

ONE FINGER WILL MEAN YOUR FAST BALL WHICH ISN'T VERY FAST ANYWAY..

TWO FINGERS WILL BE YOUR CURVE WHICH DOESN'T CURVE AT ALL..

THREE FINGERS WILL BE YOUR CHANGE-UP WHICH HASN'T FOOLED ANYONE YET...

FOUR FINGERS WAS FOR A PITCH-OUT, BUT WE WON'T USE THAT ONE
WHY NOT?
3-26

EVERYTHING YOU THROW LOOKS LIKE A PITCH-OUT!
SCHULZ

3-27

HELLO? OH, HI! HOW ARE YOU?

OH, NOTHING.. JUST PLAYING IN THIS STUPID BALL GAME..YEAH, RIGHT FIELD..

SHE DID? SHE WORE THE PINK ONE AGAIN? I CAN'T BELIEVE IT! SHE...

BONK!

SORRY.. WE WERE CUT OFF..
SCHULZ

PEANUTS
by SCHULZ

BALLOONS FOR SALE!

WHAT DO YOU THINK, MANAGER?

I CAN PLAY RIGHT FIELD AND SELL BALLOONS AT THE SAME TIME!

BALLOONS FOR SALE!

BONK!

3-28

HOW COULD I YELL AT HER? SHE GAVE ME A BALLOON!
SCHULZ

THIS IS IT, CHARLIE BROWN..LAST INNING.. TWO OUTS... AND YOU'RE UP!

ALL THE PRESSURE IS ON ME, BUT I CAN DO IT! I KNOW I CAN DO IT...
3-29

JUST DON'T GET NERVOUS..

HERE, YOU'D BETTER USE A BAT..
SCHULZ

I HIT A HOME RUN IN THE NINTH INNING, AND WE WON! I WAS THE HERO!!
YOU?!
SCHULZ
3-30

THE BALL CAME RIGHT OVER THE PLATE..
3-31

THEN, POW! YOU HIT IT OVER THE FENCE, AND WE WON THE GAME!

THEIR PITCHER WAS IN TOTAL SHOCK..

YEAH, I CAN STILL SEE THE LOOK ON HER FACE!
SCHULZ

ARE YOU THE KID WHO HIT THE HOME RUN OFF ME YESTERDAY?
4-1

WELL, I HOPE YOU'RE SATISFIED! YOU RUINED MY WHOLE LIFE!
YOU CAME CLEAR OVER HERE TO TELL ME THAT?

NO, I WAS JUST KIND OF CURIOUS TO SEE WHERE YOU LIVE..YOU PROBABLY HAVE A DOG, TOO, DON'T YOU?
SORT OF..
WHAT DO YOU MEAN, SORT OF?
SCHULZ

HEY, KID! WAIT A MINUTE! I DON'T KNOW YOUR NAME!
4-2

ROY HOBBS WAS MY GREAT-GRANDFATHER..WHEN YOU HIT THAT HOME RUN YESTERDAY, YOU RUINED MY LIFE!

I JUST MET THE GREAT-GRANDDAUGHTER OF ROY HOBBS!
I NEVER KNOW WHAT YOU'RE TALKING ABOUT..
SCHULZ

WHERE'S THE SUGAR?

MOM PUT IT IN THE REFRIGERATOR TO KEEP IT AWAY FROM THE ANTS..

JUST WHAT I NEED... COLD SUGAR..
SCHULZ
4-3

PEANUTS®
by SCHULZ

4-4

SCHULZ

WHY DON'T THEY PUT SOME OF THE GREAT OLD COMIC STRIP CHARACTERS ON STAMPS?
4-5

I THINK THAT WOULD BE A FANTASTIC IDEA..

WE COULD HAVE A SPECIAL SERIES STARTING WITH THE "YELLOW KID"

"KID." NOT BIRD!
SCHULZ

4-6

"THINGS FALL APART; THE CENTER CANNOT HOLD"

SCHULZ

WHEN CATCHERS GET HIT WITH TOO MANY FOUL BALLS, THEY GET A LITTLE WEIRD..

YOU LEAD A BORING LIFE, DID YOU KNOW THAT? YOU NEVER DO ANYTHING EXCITING

BLEAH!!

THAT WAS EXCITING..
SCHULZ
4-7

4-8

HOW ABOUT SHARING YOUR UMBRELLA?

SCHULZ

IT'S HARD TO BE A SHEPHERD WITHOUT ANY SHEEP..
4-9

OF COURSE, THERE WAS LITTLE BO-PEEP WHO HAD SOME SHEEP, BUT THEN SHE LOST THEM

BUT MAYBE IT'S BETTER TO HAVE LOST YOUR SHEEP THAN NEVER TO HAVE HAD ANY SHEEP AT ALL..

I THINK I'M CRACKING UP
SCHULZ

4-10
YOU SHOULD WRITE A SELF-HELP BOOK..

YOU KNOW, TO HELP THOSE WHO ARE LONELY AND CAN'T GO ANYPLACE..

How to be Happy Even Though You're Stuck in the Back Yard.
SCHULZ

PEANUTS
by
SCHULZ

Z

Z

YAWN

Z

4-11
Z

TOTO, I'VE A FEELING WE'RE NOT IN KANSAS ANYMORE
ROSEBUD!
SCHULZ

WHO WON THE "SPLENDID BOWL" THIS YEAR, SIR?
"SUPER BOWL," MARCIE
4-12

WHATEVER.. WAS IT A GOOD GAME?
YOU'RE NOT MUCH FOR SPORTS, ARE YOU, MARCIE?

I GUESS NOT..BUT SOMETIMES I GET A LITTLE CURIOUS...

DID ANYBODY MAKE A HOLE-IN-ONE?
SCHULZ

THIS IS MY REPORT ON RAIN

TO KEEP FROM GETTING WET, IT IS BEST TO CARRY AN UMBRELLA SIMILAR TO THIS ONE...
4-13

YES, MA'AM, I HAVE SEVERAL MORE PROPS..A PAIR OF BOOTS, THREE SANDBAGS AND VARIOUS PHOTOGRAPHS OF CLOGGED STORM DRAINS...

OKAY, LET'S FORGET THE PROPS..
SCHULZ

I SEE IT'S RAINING AGAIN, MA'AM.. MY DOG IS GOING TO GET WET...
4-14

YES, MA'AM..HE HAS A DOGHOUSE, BUT HE CAN'T GO IN IT BECAUSE HE HAS CLAUSTROPHOBIA..

I COULD GO IN THERE... I KNOW I COULD..ALL I'D HAVE TO DO IS DO IT.. I COULD JUST DO IT...

I THINK I'M GETTING WET..
SCHULZ

YOU'RE A BLOCKHEAD AND AN AIRHEAD!

YOU'RE A NOODLENECK!
4-15

YOU'RE A PUZZLEWIT AND A DIMBULB!

THE OLD WORDS STILL WORK THE BEST..
SCHULZ

DID ANYONE CALL WHILE I WAS OUT?
I DIDN'T KNOW YOU WERE OUT

WELL, DID ANYONE CALL?
CALL WHO?

ME! DID ANYONE CALL ME WHILE I WAS OUT?
WHY WOULD ANYONE CALL YOU?

AS SOON AS I'M THIRTY-FIVE, I THINK I'LL LEAVE HOME..
SCHULZ
4-16

I WONDER WHAT IT WOULD BE LIKE IF OUR ROLES WERE REVERSED..
4-17

WHAT IF YOU WERE THE MASTER AND I WERE YOUR DOG?
I THOUGHT I WAS THE MASTER..
SCHULZ

PEANUTS
by SCHULZ
"BALL FOUR!"

RATS!

WHAT DO YOU THINK?

WHEN THE FIRST PERFORMANCE OF BEETHOVEN'S NINTH SYMPHONY WAS CONCLUDED, EVERYONE IN THE AUDIENCE CHEERED...

BUT BEETHOVEN COULDN'T HEAR THEM!
4-18

I'VE ALWAYS WONDERED WHAT CATCHERS SAID TO PITCHERS WHEN THEY MET OUT ON THE MOUND
SCHULZ

DID YOU FALL IN LOVE THE FIRST TIME YOU SAW ME ?

NO, YOU DIDN'T IMPRESS ME THAT MUCH

HOW ABOUT NOW? HOW DO YOU FEEL NOW WHEN YOU LOOK AT ME?

WELL, WHEN I TWIST AROUND LIKE THIS, IT SORT OF HURTS MY NECK..

HOLD STILL.. I'M GOING TO HIT YOU WITH MY NOTEBOOK
4-19
SCHULZ

WHERE'S THE STUPID SCHOOL BUS?
I DON'T THINK IT'S COMING..
HOW LONG ARE WE SUPPOSED TO WAIT?
TWO MORE HOURS AND I'LL BE IN HIGH SCHOOL..
I'D GO BACK HOME, BUT MY MOM AND DAD HAVE PROBABLY MOVED AWAY
U.S. MAIL
4-20
SCHULZ

4-21
I DON'T THINK THE SCHOOL BUS IS EVER GOING TO COME..
I THINK THEY'VE FORGOTTEN ABOUT US..
MAYBE WE SHOULD START WALKING..
DOES ANYONE REMEMBER THE NAME OF OUR SCHOOL?
SCHULZ

I HAVEN'T WALKED TO SCHOOL IN A LONG TIME
GRAMPA SAYS HE ALWAYS WALKED TO SCHOOL..
FIVE MILES! IN ZERO WEATHER!
IN DEEP SNOW!
UPHILL!
4-22
SCHULZ

WHO'S THIS GUY?
THE PRINCIPAL.. WE HAVE TO TELL HIM WHY WE'RE LATE
TELL HIM THE BUS DIDN'T COME, AND WE WALKED ALL THE WAY
ASK HIM IF HE REMEMBERS ANY OF US..
4-23
SCHULZ

SOMETIMES I LIE AWAKE AT NIGHT, AND I ASK, "WHY AM I HERE?"

THEN A VOICE SAYS, "WHERE ARE YOU?"

"HERE," I SAY.. "WHERE IS 'HERE'?" SAYS THE VOICE..

"WAVE YOUR HAND SO I CAN SEE YOU"

THE NIGHTS ARE GETTING LONGER..
SCHULZ
4-24

PEANUTS
by SCHULZ

Z

Z
4-25

MARCIE! WHO TURNED OUT THE LIGHTS ?!

WE'VE HAD A POWER FAILURE, SIR..THE LIGHTS HAVE GONE OUT ALL OVER THE CITY..
WHY IS THIS NOTEBOOK ON MY HEAD?

TO PROTECT YOU FROM RADIATION, SIR.. WE WERE ATTACKED BY ALIENS...

WOW! THAT WAS SOME ADVENTURE, HUH, MA'AM?

HOMEWORK? NO, MA'AM.. I STARTED IT, BUT THEN WE HAD THE POWER FAILURE, AND..., WELL..

I NEVER KNOW WHAT'S GOING ON..
PRINCIPAL OFFICE
SCHULZ

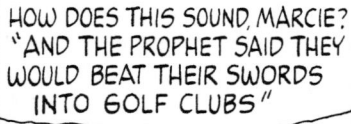

JOE GRUNGE
4-26
SCHULZ

4-27

TIRED OF PUSHING ALREADY?
SCHULZ

4-28

SCHULZ

HOW DOES THIS SOUND, MARCIE? "AND THE PROPHET SAID THEY WOULD BEAT THEIR SWORDS INTO GOLF CLUBS"

"PLOWSHARES"
4-29

TRY PLAYING EIGHTEEN HOLES WITH A PLOWSHARE, MARCIE! HA HA HA HA!!

YOU ARE EXTREMELY WEIRD, SIR..
SCHULZ

THIS NEXT GUY IS THEIR BEST HITTER..EVERY TIME HE'S UP, HE HITS A HOME RUN...

WHAT SHOULD I DO?

HOLD ON TO THE BALL UNTIL HE GOES AWAY
SCHULZ
4-30

5-1

FROM A DISTANCE, A BIRDBATH AND A SUNDIAL LOOK A LOT ALIKE..
SCHULZ

PEANUTS
by SCHULZ

EXI

THIS SHOULD BE A GOOD "TINY TOTS" CONCERT, SIR..

I HATE BEING CALLED A "TINY TOT"

WHAT ARE THEY PLAYING?

"TALES FROM THE VIENNA WOODS"

WHERE ARE THE ICE SKATERS?
SCHULZ
5/2

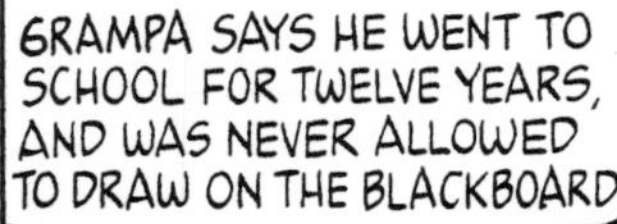
GRAMPA SAYS HE WENT TO SCHOOL FOR TWELVE YEARS, AND WAS NEVER ALLOWED TO DRAW ON THE BLACKBOARD

HE SAYS HE WAS DEPRIVED OF ONE OF THE GREAT JOYS OF LIFE..
5-3

HE SAYS SOME NIGHT AFTER A PTA MEETING, HE'S GOING TO DRAW ALL OVER ONE OF THE BLACKBOARDS..

CAN HE DRAW PRETTY WELL?
NO, ALL HE EVER DRAWS IS MICKEY MOUSE..
SCHULZ

I'M NOT GOING TO SCHOOL ANYMORE BECAUSE I ALREADY KNOW EVERYTHING I'LL EVER NEED TO KNOW..

HOW FAR AWAY IS THE MOON, WHEN WAS GEORGE WASHINGTON BORN AND WHAT'S THE FRENCH WORD FOR TOOTHPASTE?

I HOPE I HAVE A CUPCAKE IN MY LUNCH TODAY..
SCHULZ
5-4

WHAT ARE YOU WATCHING?
I DON'T KNOW
5-5
I MEAN, I KNOW WHAT I'M WATCHING, BUT I DON'T KNOW WHAT'S GOING ON
WELL, ACTUALLY, I KNOW WHAT'S GOING ON, BUT I'VE SORT OF LOST TRACK..

WHY IS BARNEY PURPLE?
SCHULZ

I'VE GOT THE NUMBERS FIGURED OUT, BUT WHO ARE THESE PEOPLE WITH THE FUNNY CLOTHES, AND WHAT GAME ARE WE PLAYING, ANYWAY?
COOKIES
I'VE GOT THE NUMBERS FIGURED OUT, BUT WHO ARE THESE PEOPLE WITH THE FUNNY CLOTHES, AND WHAT GAME ARE WE PLAYING, ANYWAY?
SCHULZ
5-6

5-7
FIRST-TIME CARD PLAYERS, SNOOPY AND RERUN, QUICKLY DISCOVER THAT THE GAME IS MORE FUN WHEN PLAYED WITH A DOUBLE DECK!
SCHULZ

TAKE A LETTER..
5-8

I'VE ALWAYS WANTED TO SAY THAT..
SCHULZ

PEANUTS®
by SCHULZ

SUPPERTIME!

JUST WHAT YOU LIKE, AND RIGHT ON TIME..

I'LL SET IT RIGHT HERE..

I EVEN BROUGHT YOU A NAPKIN

NOW YOU DON'T HAVE A THING TO COMPLAIN ABOUT

5-9
NO NAPKIN RING..
SCHULZ

WOODSTOCK! CONRAD! BILL! RAYMOND! FRED! ARE WE ALL HERE?

JUST OUT OF CURIOUSITY, HOW COME NONE OF YOU HAS A BIRD NAME?
?
5-10

NO, YOU'RE RIGHT... I WOULDN'T WANT TO BE CALLED "TWEETIE"
SCHULZ

WHERE'S YOUR STUPID DOG?
HE'S TAKING HIS TROOPS ON ANOTHER NATURE HIKE

HA! HE'LL BE LUCKY IF HE EVER FINDS HIS WAY HOME!

5-11

..AND, I HATE TO ADMIT IT, BUT IF YOU'RE LOST, THE BEST WAY TO FIND YOUR WAY HOME IS TO FOLLOW A CAT..CATS ALWAYS KNOW WHERE THEY'RE GOING..
SCHULZ

RIGHT UP AHEAD YOU'RE GOING TO SEE THE FAMOUS "BALANCING ROCK"

"BALANCING ROCK" HAS BEEN PERCHED ON THIS CLIFF FOR TEN MILLION YEARS, AND...
5-12

I GUESS WE SHOULD HAVE COME YESTERDAY..
SCHULZ

HERE'S A REAL TREAT FOR ALL OF US... A CHANCE TO DRINK PURE WATER FROM A COOL MOUNTAIN STREAM..

5-13
NO, FRED.. I DIDN'T BRING ANY STRAWS!
SCHULZ

I HAVE A SURPRISE FOR YOU..
5-14

BEFORE WE ALL GO TO SLEEP, I'M GOING TO READ A LITTLE FROM MY FAMOUS NOVEL, "IT WAS A DARK AND STORMY NIGHT"

Z
Z
Z
Z
Z
SCHULZ

YOUR STUPID DOG DIDN'T COME HOME LAST NIGHT
NO, I GUESS HE'S CAMPING OUT WITH HIS TROOPS..

GATHER 'ROUND, MEN, AND WATCH ME FLIP THESE PANCAKES!

SORRY, CONRAD
SCHULZ
5-15

PEANUTS
by SCHULZ
SHOW HIM HOW, BIG BROTHER!

BRUSH HIM BACK!

STRIKE HIM OUT, BIG BROTHER! YOU CAN DO IT! STRIKE HIM OUT!!

5-16

DID YOU STRIKE HIM OUT?
SCHULZ

WELL, I SEE YOU'RE BACK FROM YOUR CAMPING TRIP..

I HOPE YOU ENJOYED IT AS MUCH AS THE BIRDS..

I DON'T KNOW.. I HATE CHIRPING AROUND THE CAMPFIRE..
SCHULZ
5-17

LEND ME YOUR PEN, WILL YOU, MARCIE?

5-18
THEN LET ME HAVE YOUR PENCIL..

TIME OUT, MA'AM, FOR AN EQUIPMENT CHANGE!
SCHULZ

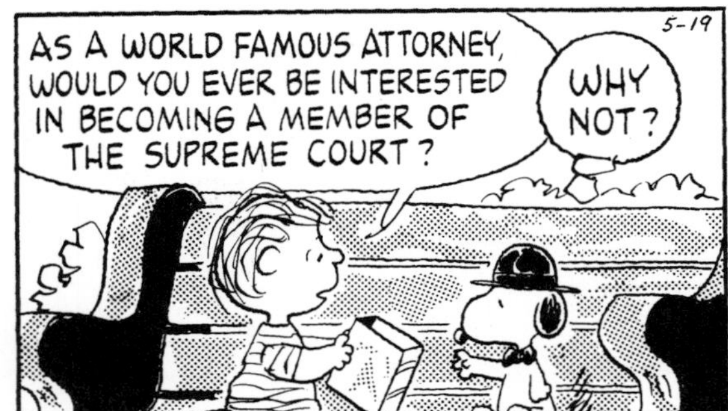
5-19
AS A WORLD FAMOUS ATTORNEY, WOULD YOU EVER BE INTERESTED IN BECOMING A MEMBER OF THE SUPREME COURT?
WHY NOT?

OF COURSE, YOU'D HAVE TO MOVE TO WASHINGTON..
WHERE'S THAT?
SCHULZ

Dear Mr. President,
Apparently there is soon to be an opening on the Supreme Court.

I would like to recommend a friend of mine who is a world famous attorney.

WHERE SHOULD I TELL HIM YOU WENT TO LAW SCHOOL?
YOU'D BETTER SKIP THAT PART..
SCHULZ
5-20

5-21
I CAN SEE YOU NOW SITTING ON THE BENCH OF THE SUPREME COURT..THEY'D PROBABLY PUT YOU RIGHT NEXT TO JUDGE SANDRA DAY O'CONNOR..
IS SHE CUTE?
SCHULZ

A JUDGE ON THE SUPREME COURT?! THAT STUPID DOG COULDN'T BE A JUDGE ON A TENNIS COURT!
AU CONTRAIRE! HE IS AN ATTORNEY WITH THE HIGHEST OF REPUTATIONS!
WHAT HAPPENED TO ALL THE COOKIES?
SCHULZ
5-22

PEANUTS®
by SCHULZ

AAUGH! I GOT A CRAMP IN MY FOOT!

OW! OUCH! OW!

AAUGH! MY LEG IS ASLEEP!

5-23

?

SCHULZ

OKAY, LET'S SAY THE PRESIDENT HAS APPOINTED YOU TO THE SUPREME COURT...

NOW, YOU'RE FACING THE SENATE JUDICIARY COMMITTEE, AND SENATOR BIDEN ASKS YOU A TOUGH QUESTION.. HOW WILL YOU RESPOND?

WOOF!

5-24
I THINK YOU'RE IN!
SCHULZ

HERE'S THE WORLD FAMOUS ATTORNEY ON HIS WAY TO WASHINGTON TO TAKE HIS SEAT ON THE SUPREME COURT..

WHAT'S THIS? A FUNNY LOOKING DOG DRESSED UP LIKE AN ATTORNEY!

5-25
WHAP!
"THE LAW IS EVERMORE THE LEADER IN SOCIETY"
SCHULZ

YOUR STUPID DOG JUST LEFT FOR WASHINGTON
HE WHAT?

LINUS TALKED HIM INTO TRYING OUT FOR THE SUPREME COURT

SNOOPY! COME BACK!

HERE'S THE WORLD FAMOUS ATTORNEY ON HIS WAY TO WASHINGTON TO TAKE HIS SEAT ON THE SUPREME COURT..

I DIDN'T EVEN GET TO THE JUDICIARY COMMITTEE..
5-26
SCHULZ

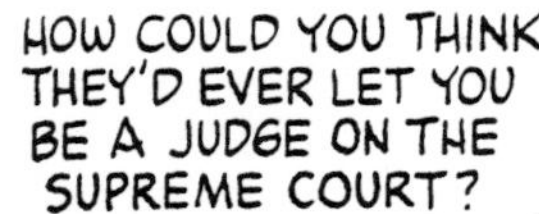
HOW COULD YOU THINK THEY'D EVER LET YOU BE A JUDGE ON THE SUPREME COURT?

YOU CAN'T EVEN DECIDE IF YOU'LL HAVE YOUR SUPPER IN THE RED DISH OR THE YELLOW DISH..
5-27

OR YOUR DRINKING WATER IN THE GREEN DISH OR THE BLUE DISH!

THOSE DISHES SHOULD ALL BE THE SAME COLOR..
SCHULZ

5-28
ONE FINGER WILL MEAN A FAST BALL, TWO FINGERS A CURVE, AND THREE FINGERS WILL MEAN TURN AROUND AND TRY TO HIT YOUR RIGHT-FIELDER IN THE HEAD WITH THE BALL!
GAME CALLED ON ACCOUNT OF DARKNESS! WHERE'D EVERYBODY GO? I CAN'T SEE A THING!
SCHULZ

WHAT IF I DECIDED TO PLANT A GARDEN?

YOU MEAN DIG UP THE SOIL, PULL ALL THE WEEDS, PLANT THE SEEDS, PULL SOME MORE WEEDS, WATER THE SEEDS, AND PULL SOME MORE WEEDS?
5-29

WHAT IF I DECIDE TO CHANGE MY MIND?
SCHULZ

PEANUTS®
by SCHULZ

BONSOIR, MONSIEUR FAMOUS FLYING ACE OF WORLD WAR I

DO YOU SEE WHO'S SITTING OVER THERE TONIGHT? IT'S THE RED BARON!

I THINK HE WANTS TO BUY YOU A DRINK..

TELL HIM I'LL HAVE A ROOT BEER, AND WE'LL DRINK A TOAST!
OUI, MONSIEUR..

5-30

VERY FUNNY, RED BARON!
SCHULZ

WHEN YOU DIE, ARE YOU EVER ALLOWED TO COME BACK?

ONLY IF YOU HAD YOUR HAND STAMPED..
5-31
SCHULZ

TELL ME, AS A WORLD FAMOUS SURGEON, ARE MOST OF YOUR PATIENTS ANIMALS OR HUMAN BEINGS?

BOTH, I GUESS..

I USED TO OPERATE ON FISH, BUT FISH NEVER HAVE ANY MONEY
6-1
SCHULZ

SLEEP WELL, OL' PAL..TOMORROW WILL BE A NEW DAY, AND WE NEVER KNOW WHAT EXCITEMENT LIES AHEAD..
ACTUALLY, I CAN'T TELL ONE DAY FROM THE OTHER..
6-2
SCHULZ

HOW ABOUT THIS, MARCIE? IT LOOKS LIKE SHE GAVE ME AN "A" IN EVERY SUBJECT...

6-3

YOU'RE RIGHT.. HER "D-MINUSES" DO LOOK LIKE "A'S"
SCHULZ

YOU KNOW WHAT I THINK, CHUCK? I THINK YOU GET BETTER GRADES IF YOU'RE CUTE..

I'LL BET MY TEACHER WOULD HAVE GIVEN ME ALL "A'S" IF I LOOKED LIKE THIS..
6-4

I LIKED YOU FINE THE OTHER WAY..
THANK YOU, CHUCK

BOY, THAT HURTS YOUR EYES..
SCHULZ

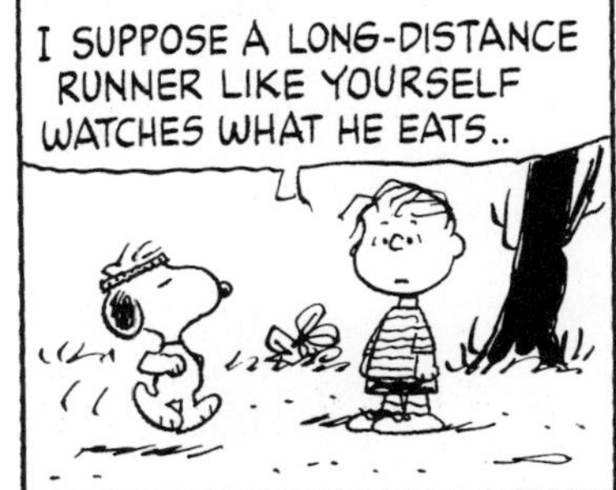
I SUPPOSE A LONG-DISTANCE RUNNER LIKE YOURSELF WATCHES WHAT HE EATS..

ABSOLUTELY
6-5

AFTER I'M DONE, I ALWAYS EAT A POWER DOUGHNUT..
SCHULZ

JUNE 6, 1944, "TO REMEMBER"

SCHULZ

MY GRAMPA SAYS THOSE WERE THE GOOD DAYS..

6-7
WHAT DAYS ?

HE DOESN'T KNOW WHAT DAYS, BUT HE'S SURE THOSE WERE THE GOOD DAYS..
SCHULZ

6-8

THAT WAS FUN!
STUPID DOG!
SCHULZ

I'LL JUST SIT HERE, AND LET YOU DIVIDE THE COOKIES BETWEEN US..
DOGS CAN'T COUNT
SCHULZ
6-9

I'M SORRY I'M LATE WITH YOUR SUPPER.. I STOPPED TO ADMIRE THE SUNSET..

THERE WAS A GLOW IN THE SKY LIKE I'VE NEVER SEEN BEFORE..
6-10

I DON'T THINK THERE'S A WORD THAT DESCRIBES HOW IT CAN MAKE YOU FEEL...

HUNGRY!
SCHULZ

SO HERE I AM RIDING ON THE BACK OF MY MOM'S BICYCLE..

THIS SHOULD BE A GOOD TRIP IF SHE STEERS STRAIGHT...

..AND IF OUR FRONT WHEEL DOESN'T GO DOWN THAT..

6-11
..GRATE!
SCHULZ

ALL RIGHT, TROOPS..BEFORE YOU GO TO SLEEP, I WANT TO HEAR SOME BEDTIME PRAYERS..
6-12

I DIDN'T KNOW THEY HAD THEOLOGICAL DIFFERENCES..
SCHULZ

PEANUTS
by SCHULZ
CHOMP CHOMP

NO, NOT AT ALL..

NO, MA'AM..I CAN'T SEE THE QUESTION ON THE BLACKBOARD

BUT DON'T DESPAIR, MA'AM..I'M EATING CARROT CAKE!

YES, MA'AM.. A LITTLE MID-MORNING SNACK..

CARROTS ARE GOOD FOR YOUR EYES.. YOU KNEW THAT, DIDN'T YOU, MA'AM?

THERE! THAT WAS GREAT!

OKAY, NOW LET'S TAKE ANOTHER LOOK AT THAT QUESTION ON THE BLACKBOARD...
6-13

I CAN SEE IT! THE CARROT CAKE DID ITS JOB!

YES, MA'AM, I CAN SEE THE QUESTION, BUT I STILL DON'T KNOW THE ANSWER..

DON'T SIGH, MA'AM..EATING CARROT CAKE IN THE MORNING MAKES YOU WEIRD..
SCHULZ

6-14
SOMETIMES, CHUCK, I WONDER IF YOU EVER REALIZE JUST HOW EMBARRASSING THIS CAN BE..
SCHULZ

IT'S A BEAUTIFUL SIGHT, ISN'T IT?

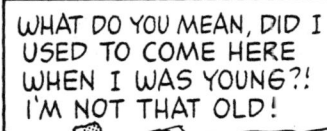

WHAT DO YOU MEAN, DID I USED TO COME HERE WHEN I WAS YOUNG?! I'M NOT THAT OLD!
6-15

NO, I NEVER KNEW BILLY THE KID!
SCHULZ

WHEN I WENT INTO TOWN TO PLAY GOLF, THEY ASKED ME WHAT MY HANDICAP IS...
6-16

I SAID MY HANDICAP IS I'M A DOG..

THEN THEY SAID DOGS AREN'T ALLOWED ON THE COURSE..

SO I THOUGHT MAYBE I'D SUE..

BUT DOGS AREN'T ALLOWED IN THE COURTHOUSE..
SCHULZ

BONK
6-17

LUCY, YOU'RE THE WORST PLAYER IN THE HISTORY OF THE GAME!

YOU CAN'T PROVE THAT! YOU SHOULD NEVER SAY THINGS THAT YOU CAN'T PROVE!

IN ALL PROBABILITY, YOU ARE THE WORST PLAYER IN THE HISTORY OF THE GAME!

I CAN ACCEPT THAT..
SCHULZ

DID YOU KNOW THAT BLACKBEARD, THE PIRATE, BURIED ALL HIS GOLD HERE IN THE DESERT?
6-18

AND THAT BLACKBEARD ONCE SPENT THE NIGHT IN A MOTEL IN NEEDLES? THAT'S WHAT SOMEONE TOLD ME..

YOU DON'T BELIEVE ANYTHING, DO YOU?
SCHULZ

Dear Pen Pal, How have you been?
WHY DO YOU HAVE A PEN PAL?

TO LEARN ABOUT OTHER CULTURES... HE TELLS ME ABOUT HIMSELF, AND I TELL HIM ABOUT ME..

WHY WOULD ANYONE WANT TO HEAR ABOUT YOU?

Some days I feel like I'm writing uphill.
SCHULZ
6-19

HERE, BOY!
PEANUTS®
by SCHULZ
"BOY"?

GET IT!

GET IT, BOY! GET THE BALL!

THAT'S THE WAY! GOOD DOG!

GET IT, PAL!

THAT'S THE WAY! BRING IT HERE!

GET IT, BOY! GET THE STICK!

THATTA BOY! BRING IT BACK!
6-20

WHAT DID YOU DO FOR YOUR DAD FOR FATHER'S DAY, CHARLIE BROWN?
I LET HIM PLAY WITH MY DOG..
SCHULZ

HEY, KID..REMEMBER ME? I'M ROY HOBBS' GREAT-GRANDDAUGHTER

I KNOW.. I'M VERY IMPRESSED
THE LAST TIME WE PLAYED, YOU HIT A HOME RUN OFF ME, AND RUINED MY LIFE!
6-21

I WAS JUST LUCKY
I SUPPOSE YOU THINK YOU'RE GONNA DO IT AGAIN..

WHAT'RE YOU TRYIN' TO DO NEXT, RUIN MY AFTERLIFE?
SCHULZ

YOU'RE UP NEXT, CHARLIE BROWN..YOU CAN HIT THIS PITCHER! THE LAST TIME YOU FACED HER, YOU HIT A HOME RUN!
6-22

YOU CAN DO IT! YOU'RE THE HERO TYPE!

OR THE GOAT TYPE..
SCHULZ

THAT ROUND-HEADED KID IS UP NEXT, ISN'T HE?
6-23

SO WHAT? HE WAS JUST LUCKY THE LAST TIME WE PLAYED...

YOU'RE ROY HOBBS' GREAT-GRANDDAUGHTER, AREN'T YOU? WELL, SHOW 'IM WHO YOU ARE!

THROW IT IN HERE, ROYANNE!
ROYANNE?
SCHULZ

STRIKE ONE!

C'MON, CHARLIE BROWN! SHE'S NO PITCHER! SHE'S ONLY A GIRL!
ONLY A GIRL?!

WELL, I'M ONLY YOUR SISTER, YOU BLOCKHEAD!!

HEY, I THOUGHT I FELT A DROP OF RAIN..

I DID! IT'S RAINING!
STRIKE TWO!

HA! YOU'RE DOOMED, KID! YOU'RE GONNA STRIKE OUT!!

NO, I'M GONNA DROWN..

TWO STRIKES ON THAT ROUND-HEADED KID, AND IT STARTS RAINING!
MAYBE IT'LL STOP SOON..
YOU CAN GET A HIT, CHARLIE BROWN..DON'T LET THAT GIRL STRIKE YOU OUT!
SHE THROWS PRETTY HARD..
I'M A HOUSE DOG.. HOUSE DOGS AREN'T SUPPOSED TO GET WET

PEANUTS
by SCHULZ

OKAY, TEAM.. WE'RE UP TO BAT!

SO I'VE BEEN WONDERING..

WHICH IS MORE IMPORTANT? WHICH IS THE GREATER ACCOMPLISHMENT?

WHICH WOULD YOU RATHER DO.. WRITE "WAR AND PEACE" LIKE LEO TOLSTOY...

..OR HIT SIXTY-ONE HOME RUNS LIKE ROGER MARIS?
6-27

STRIKE THREE!

I PROBABLY WON'T WRITE "WAR AND PEACE" EITHER..
SCHULZ

OKAY, KID, IT'S STOPPED RAINING, AND YOU GOT TWO STRIKES AGAINST YOU!

TIME OUT! ONE OF MY PLAYERS WANTS TO TALK TO ME...

THEY'RE HAVING A CONFERENCE, AREN'T THEY? THEY'RE PLANNING SOME CLEVER STRATEGY.. I JUST FEEL IT...

6-28

NO, LAST NIGHT YOU HAD YOUR SUPPER IN THE RED DISH AND WATER IN THE YELLOW DISH..
SCHULZ

CRACK!

HE HIT IT! CHARLIE BROWN HIT IT! THE BALL IS GOING TO THE FENCE! RUN, CHARLIE BROWN! RUN!
OH, NO! THE WORLD IS COMING TO AN END! I ALWAYS KNEW IT WOULD END THIS WAY!
6-29
SCHULZ

CHARLIE BROWN IS ROUNDING FIRST! HE'S ROUNDING SECOND! HE'S ROUNDING THIRD...

BUT ROY HOBBS' GREAT-GRANDDAUGHTER HAS THE BALL!! SHE'S BLOCKING THE PLATE!!!

6-30
SCHULZ

SLIDE, CHARLIE BROWN, SLIDE!!

7-1
SCHULZ

YOU DID IT, CHARLIE BROWN! YOU HIT ANOTHER HOME RUN, AND WE WON THE GAME!
YOU MEAN I WAS SAFE?
I'M ROY HOBBS' GREAT-GRANDDAUGHTER.. WHERE AM I ? WHAT HAPPENED?
YOU WERE BLOCKING THE PLATE, SWEETIE.. HERE, I COULD ONLY FIND ONE SHOE..
7-2
SCHULZ

WELL, YOU DID IT AGAIN, DIDN'T YOU? YOU HIT ANOTHER HOME RUN, AND RUINED MY LIFE!
I WAS LUCKY

YOU ALMOST KILLED ME WHEN YOU SLID INTO HOME..
YOU WERE BLOCKING THE PLATE, SWEETIE..

I STILL CAN'T FIND MY OTHER SHOE...
I'M SORRY
7-3

I HATE GOING THE REST OF MY LIFE WEARING ONLY ONE SHOE
SCHULZ

PEANUTS
by
SCHULZ

YAWN

Z
Z

Z
Z

7-4
Z
Z

Z
Z

Z
Z
SCHULZ

THIS WOULD BE A MUCH BETTER WORLD IF DOGS COULD FLY, TOO..
7-5

IMAGINE A WARM SUMMER NIGHT...

AND OVERHEAD, A SKY FILLED WITH DOGS BARKING
SCHULZ

YOU KNOW HOW EVERYONE LIKES TO SEE GEESE FLYING ACROSS THE FACE OF A FULL MOON?
7-6

IF DOGS COULD FLY, WOULDN'T IT BE NEAT TO LOOK UP AND SEE A SAINT BERNARD FLYING ACROSS THE FACE OF THE MOON?

WELL, MAYBE NOT..
SCHULZ

ARE YOU AWAKE?
WHO WANTS TO KNOW?

7-7
I'M YOUR BROTHER... REMEMBER ME?

DO YOU HAVE ANY IDENTIFICATION?
SCHULZ

7-8

YES, I AGREE.. IT TAKES COURAGE TO SAIL IN UNCHARTED WATERS..

I'M NOT SURE I WANT TO GO TO CAMP..

WELL, YOU'D BETTER MAKE UP YOUR MIND... THE BUS LEAVES IN FIVE MINUTES!
7-9

I'LL BE THERE IN SIX MINUTES..

NO, SIR.. MY SISTER WON'T BE COMING TO CAMP THIS YEAR.. SHE MISSED THE BUS... BUT I'M HERE!

YES, SIR.. A YEAR AGO.. LAST PLACE IN THE SACK RACE.. UH HUH.. THAT WAS ME..
7-10

NO, I UNDERSTAND... YOU HAVE A LOT OF CAMPERS COME THROUGH HERE..
SCHULZ

PEANUTS
by SCHULZ
"'AND I WISH YOU WOULDN'T KEEP APPEARING AND VANISHING,' SAID ALICE"

"'YOU MAKE ONE QUITE GIDDY'"

"'ALL RIGHT,' SAID THE CAT; AND THIS TIME IT VANISHED SLOWLY, ENDING WITH THE GRIN..'

I CAN DO THAT..

READ SOMETHING ELSE...QUICK!
SCHULZ
7-11

CALLING HOME, CHARLIE BROWN?

I THOUGHT I'D LET EVERYONE KNOW THAT I GOT HERE TO CAMP SAFELY..

" THANK YOU FOR CALLING THE BROWN RESIDENCE.. IF YOU KNOW THE FOUR DIGIT EXTENSION OF THE PARTY YOU ARE TRYING TO REACH, YOU MAY DIAL IT NOW.. IF YOU ARE CALLING YOUR SISTER, PRESS THREE.. IF YOU HAVE A ROTARY DIAL TELEPHONE, PLEASE HOLD FOR THE NEXT AVAILABLE PERSON... "
SCHULZ
7-12

HELLO? OH, IS THIS YOU, BIG BROTHER?
7-13

YOU'RE AT CAMP, AND I'M NOT! HA HA HA HA HA!!

NEVER CALL HOME!
SCHULZ

HI! MY NAME IS ETHAN.. I JUST GOT BACK FROM "CRAFTS"

WE'VE BEEN LEARNING HOW TO MAKE BOWS AND ARROWS LIKE THE INDIANS..
7-14

THIS IS THE ARROW I MADE..
THAT'S AN INDIAN ARROW?

SURE, WITHOUT IT, THEY WOULDN'T KNOW WHICH WAY THEY WERE GOING..
SCHULZ

WHAT DO YOU WANT TO BE WHEN YOU GROW UP, ETHAN?

A NEWSPAPER COLUMNIST..

I HAVE VERY STRONG OPINIONS ABOUT EVERYTHING
7-15

THAT'S A STUPID LOOKING SHIRT YOU'RE WEARING..
SCHULZ

CARL SAGAN SAYS THERE ARE A HUNDRED BILLION STARS IN OUR GALAXY, AND THERE ARE A HUNDRED BILLION GALAXIES, AND EACH GALAXY CONTAINS A HUNDRED BILLION STARS! SORT OF PUTS THINGS IN PERSPECTIVE, DOESN'T IT CHARLIE BROWN?
I MISS MY DOG..
7-16
SCHULZ

HI, SALLY.. I'M COMING HOME THIS AFTERNOON...

HAS MY DOG MISSED ME?
7-17

OH, YES.. HE'S BEEN WAITING FOR YOU...

WELCOME HOME, ROUND-HEADED KID!
SCHULZ

PEANUTS
by SCHULZ

BAM!
BAM!

ARE YOU UPSET, LITTLE FRIEND? HAVE YOU BEEN LYING AWAKE WORRYING? WELL, DON'T WORRY.. I'M HERE

I'M HERE TO GIVE YOU REASSURANCE.. EVERYTHING IS ALL RIGHT...

THE FLOOD WATERS WILL RECEDE.. THE FAMINE WILL END.. THE SUN WILL SHINE TOMORROW...
7-18

AND I WILL ALWAYS BE HERE TO TAKE CARE OF YOU!

BE REASSURED!

WHO REASSURES THE REASSURER?
SCHULZ

I KNOW IT'S HOT, MEN, BUT LET'S KEEP GOING..

NOT TOO FAR AHEAD IS AN OASIS WHERE THERE'LL BE LOTS OF WATER...

7-19
SCHULZ

7-20

IT IS SAID THAT WHEN DOGS DRINK FROM THE RIVER NILE, THEY DO IT WHILE RUNNING SO AS NOT TO BE SEIZED BY CROCODILES..

I FEEL RIDICULOUS
SCHULZ

?
JUST SPIT THEM OUT..
7-21

THOSE ARE BUTTONS..THEY KEEP THE WATERMELON FROM FALLING APART..

HE NEVER BELIEVES ANYTHING I TELL HIM
SCHULZ

FALLING ROCK

7-22
FALLING THINGS
SCHULZ

SO HERE I AM LEFT TO GUARD THE CAR WHILE THE FAMILY GOES SHOPPING..
7-23

ANYONE WHO COMES NEAR THIS VEHICLE WILL MEET A SNARLING TORNADO!

ON THE OTHER HAND, FOR TWO COOKIES THEY CAN HAVE THE CAR..
SCHULZ

7-24

SCHULZ

PEANUTS
by SCHULZ

THIS IS KIND OF INTERESTING

"SOMETIMES WHEN A DOG IS ABOUT TO GO TO SLEEP, IT WILL TURN AROUND IN A CIRCLE BEFORE LYING DOWN.."

"THIS HABIT GOES BACK TO THE DOG'S WILD ANCESTORS WHO STAMPED DOWN THE GRASS TO FORM A NESTLIKE BED.."

7-25

WHAT DOES IT SAY ABOUT WAKING UP?
SCHULZ

7-26
Z

YOU KNOW WHAT'S WRONG WITH YOUR STORY? IT'S UNBELIEVABLY BORING!

A PERSON COULD FALL ASLEEP READING IT..

I FELL ASLEEP WRITING IT!
SCHULZ

I THINK YOU TAKE THIS GAME TOO SERIOUSLY, CHARLIE BROWN...
7-27

YOU PUT TOO MUCH STRESS ON YOURSELF..

YOU'RE PROBABLY RIGHT, LUCY.. THANKS FOR REMINDING ME..

TRY TO GET THE BALL OVER THE PLATE! YOU THINK WE'RE OUT HERE FOR THE FUN OF IT?!
SCHULZ

He was tough.
He was mean.
7-28

They called him "Macho Beagle."

He carried his own felt pen.
SCHULZ

OKAY, SHOOT!

7-29

YOU DIDN'T SAY, "NICE TRY"
SCHULZ

GUESS WHAT, MARCIE.. I'VE BEEN DOING A LITTLE SUMMER READING..

MAYBE YOU CAN HELP ME.. WHY DID VANNA WHITE TAKE THE CARAMELED APPLE FROM THE WITCH?

"SNOW" WHITE, SIR.. AND IT WAS A PLAIN APPLE..
7-30

PRETTY PROFOUND STORY, HUH, MARCIE?
SCHULZ

PSYCHIATRIC HELP 5¢
HOW DO I KNOW IF THE ADVICE YOU'RE GOING TO GIVE ME WILL BE ANY GOOD?
THE DOCTOR IS IN
7-31

ANY ADVICE YOU GET HERE IS GUARANTEED TO BE RIGHT ON TARGET..
THE DOCTOR IS IN

ALL RIGHT, I'LL TAKE A CHANCE...

SIT UP STRAIGHT! YOU'RE SLOUCHING!
SCHULZ
THE DOCTOR IS IN

PEANUTS®
by SCHULZ

MMMM!

BEAUTIFUL!

?

NO, I DON'T THINK SO..
8-1

?
OKAY, TAKE A LOOK IF YOU WANT TO..

I KNEW YOU WOULDN'T BE ABLE TO SEE HOW THEY GET THE JELLY INSIDE THE DOUGHNUT..
SCHULZ

DO YOU THINK IT'S POSSIBLE TO RIDE CLEAR ACROSS THE LAKE ON A BEACH BALL?

I DOUBT IT, WHY?
I WAS JUST WONDERING..
SCHULZ
8-2

DEAR GRANDMA, I AM DICTATING THIS LETTER TO MY SISTER SALLY WHO IS STUDYING SHORTHAND...

8-3

MAYBE YOU'D BETTER JUST CALL HER ON THE PHONE..
SCHULZ

SOMETIMES I LIE AWAKE AT NIGHT, AND I ASK MYSELF, "IS THIS ALL THERE IS?"

THEN I HEAR A VOICE THAT SAYS..
8-4

"WHAT KIND OF A QUESTION IS THAT?"
SCHULZ

IF YOU PAID SEVENTEEN DOLLARS FOR A MAILBOX AND YOU ONLY GOT ONE LOVE LETTER, IT WOULD STILL BE WORTH IT...
8-5
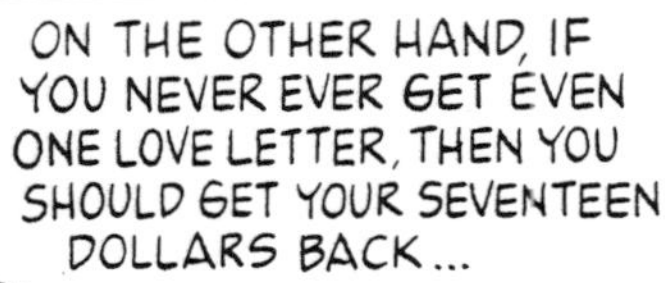
ON THE OTHER HAND, IF YOU NEVER EVER GET EVEN ONE LOVE LETTER, THEN YOU SHOULD GET YOUR SEVENTEEN DOLLARS BACK...

I'D LIKE TO SPEAK TO THE MANAGER, PLEASE..
SCHULZ

DID YOU KNOW OUR NAME IS IN THE PHONE BOOK?
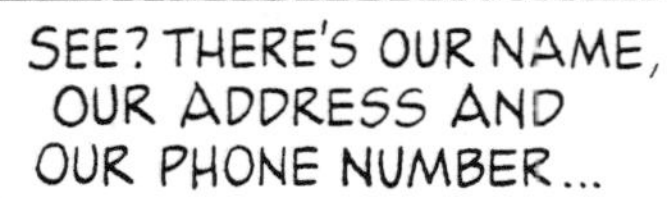
SEE? THERE'S OUR NAME, OUR ADDRESS AND OUR PHONE NUMBER...

8-6

YOU NEVER TOLD ME WE WERE FAMOUS..
SCHULZ

IF OUR NAME IS IN THE PHONE BOOK, WHY ISN'T OUR NAME IN THE "OLD TESTAMENT"?
8-7

TRY GENESIS 30:32

"..AND ALL THE BROWN CATTLE AMONG THE SHEEP"

WOW!
SCHULZ

TIME OUT!
PEANUTS®
by SCHULZ

LISTEN TO ME, CHARLIE BROWN..

I THINK YOU SHOULD THROW NOTHING BUT FASTBALLS TO THIS NEXT GUY...

AND WATCH THE KID ON SECOND.. HE'S BEEN TAKING A BIG LEAD...

8-8
ANYTHING ELSE?

I THINK IT BROKE BEETHOVEN'S HEART WHEN GIULIETTA GUICCIARDI MARRIED COUNT VON GALLENBERG..

CATCHERS HAVE A LOT ON THEIR MINDS..
SCHULZ

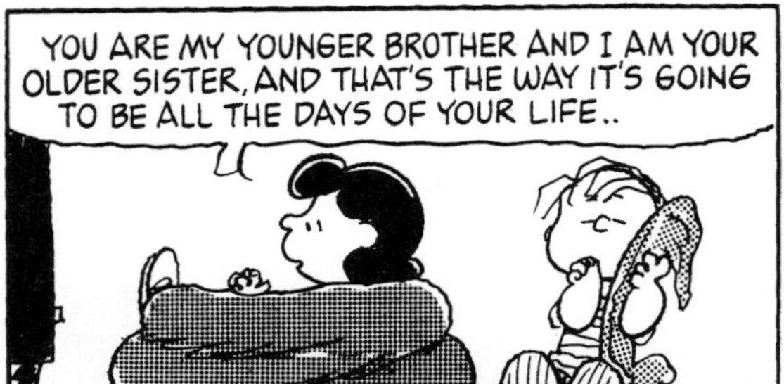
YOU ARE MY YOUNGER BROTHER AND I AM YOUR OLDER SISTER, AND THAT'S THE WAY IT'S GOING TO BE ALL THE DAYS OF YOUR LIFE..

8-9
..AND DON'T TELL ME YOU NEVER THINK ABOUT IT..
SCHULZ

THE SUN IS IN YOUR EYES?

WELL, PUT ON SOME SUNGLASSES, OR WEAR A HAT OR SIT UNDER AN UMBRELLA..

8-10
..OR DO ALL THREE..
SCHULZ

YES, MA'AM..DO YOU HAVE ANY BOOKS HERE IN YOUR LIBRARY WHERE A DOG TAKES OVER THE WHOLE WORLD?
SCHULZ

8-11
WELL, I THINK NOW YOU'VE GOT ONE..

SCHOOL STARTS IN
FOUR WEEKS!!

DETAILS AT
ELEVEN..

YES, SIR.. WE'D LIKE TO
BUY SOME SCHOOL SUPPLIES

THINGS LIKE PAPER
AND PENCILS..

AND LOTS OF
ERASERS..

YES, SIR.. YOU WANT TO
KNOW WHY WE'RE BUYING
OUR SCHOOL SUPPLIES
SO EARLY?

TELL HIM WE'RE TRYING
TO CREATE THE ILLUSION
THAT WE'RE ANXIOUS
TO BECOME EDUCATED..

WE JUST LIKE
TO BE PREPARED

MY ANSWER
WAS BETTER

PEANUTS®
by
SCHULZ

8-15

WHY CAN'T I HAVE A NORMAL DOG LIKE EVERYONE ELSE?
SCHULZ

NOW, GET OUT THERE IN RIGHT FIELD, AND CONCENTRATE!

THINK ABOUT WHAT YOU'RE DOING..

KEEP YOUR MIND ON THE GAME..
8-16

KEEP YOUR HEAD OUT OF THE CLOUDS..

SCHULZ

ROYANNE! WHAT A SURPRISE!

I NEED TO TALK TO YOU, CHARLES..DO YOU HAVE TIME TO GO GET A CHOCOLATE SUNDAE?
8-17

OKAY, ROYANNE, WHAT'S UP?

DO YOU LIKE ME, CHARLES?
OH, GOOD GRIEF!
SCHULZ

I HAVE TO TELL YOU SOMETHING, CHARLES.. BUT FIRST, I WANT TO KNOW IF YOU LIKE ME...

WELL, SURE, I LIKE YOU, ROYANNE.. BUT I DON'T REALLY KNOW YOU..I MEAN, OUR TEAM PLAYED YOUR TEAM A COUPLE OF TIMES..

AND, OF COURSE, I HIT THOSE TWO HOME RUNS, AND..
8-18

THAT'S WHAT I HAVE TO CONFESS, CHARLES..I COULD HAVE STRUCK YOU OUT IF I HAD WANTED TO!
SCHULZ

YOU LET ME HIT THOSE HOME RUNS?!
8-19

I HAD TO, CHARLES..YOU LOOKED CUTE STANDING THERE AT THE PLATE..
I DIDN'T WANT TO LOOK CUTE!!

HOW ABOUT PATHETIC?
I CAN'T STAND IT!
SCHULZ

WHY DID YOU TELL ME YOU LET ME HIT THOSE HOME RUNS? I LIKED BEING A HERO..
8-20

I'M ROY HOBBS' GREAT-GRANDDAUGHTER.. I HAVE A REPUTATION
ROY HOBBS WAS A FICTIONAL CHARACTER

WHAT?!
DIDN'T YOU KNOW THAT?

MY LIFE IS RUINED..
WHEN YOUR LIFE HAS BEEN RUINED, YOU SHOULD LIE UNDER A TREE ALL AFTERNOON..
SCHULZ

SHE ASKED YOU TO GO OUT FOR A CHOCOLATE SUNDAE?

UH HUH.. AND THEN SHE CONFESSED THAT SHE HAD LET ME HIT THOSE HOME RUNS! I WAS CRUSHED!
8-21

I WAS HUMILIATED!

AND THEN SHE LET ME PAY FOR THE CHOCOLATE SUNDAES!
SCHULZ

PEANUTS
by SCHULZ

I THINK THAT'S HER HOUSE THERE..

HI, CHUCK! THANKS FOR BRINGING YOUR DOG OVER..

MY DAD AND I ARE GOING TO BE GONE OVERNIGHT SO WE NEED A WATCHDOG TO GUARD THE HOUSE..

NOW, AROUND HERE IS THE BACKDOOR...

AND THIS IS THE ENTRANCE TO THE GARAGE..IF ANYONE COMES AROUND, HE SHOULD BARK LIKE MAD!

IT'LL PROBABLY BE BEST IF HE JUST STANDS GUARD HERE AT THE FRONT OF THE HOUSE, AND...
Z
8-22

Z

YOU SURE KNOW HOW TO GET OUT OF THINGS, DON'T YOU?
SCHULZ

HORSES ARE RELATIVELY EASY TO TRAIN..MULES ARE EASIER TO TRAIN THAN DONKEYS..IT TAKES PATIENCE TO TRAIN A DONKEY...A MULE IS ONE-HALF DONKEY AND ONE-HALF HORSE..
DON'T ALWAYS FEEL IT'S NECESSARY TO MAKE CONVERSATION, MARCIE..
8-23
SCHULZ

MISS DAVIS IS GOING TO BE SURPRISED WHEN SHE GETS THIS BOOK REPORT..

MISS DAVIS QUIT TEACHING TWO YEARS AGO..SHE GOT MARRIED, AND HAS A NEW BABY

MAYBE I COULD ATTACH A "CONGRATULATIONS" CARD TO THE REPORT..
SCHULZ
8/24

YOU KNOW WHAT WE SHOULD DO, MARCIE? WE SHOULD SIGN UP FOR RIDING LESSONS..

ON HORSES?

THERE AREN'T ANY ZEBRAS AROUND HERE, MARCIE..
8-25
SCHULZ

8-26

YOU'RE LATE.. WE'VE ALREADY STARTED EATING
THERE WAS HEAVY FIGHTING OVER ST. MIHIEL..

LINUS IS HAVING DINNER WITH US TONIGHT

WHY IS HE LOOKING AT ME SO FUNNY?
I'M NOT USED TO EATING WITH THE ENLISTED MEN
SCHULZ

IF YOU'RE GOING TO BE FLYING OVER PARIS, COULD I HITCH A RIDE?
8-27

IT'S AGAINST REGULATIONS, BUT I SUPPOSE WE CAN DO IT..

IS IT VERY FAR?
NO, THERE'S PARIS NOW..

HAVE A GOOD TIME!
SCHULZ

HEY, CHUCK..YOUR CRAZY DOG ALMOST KILLED ME!
8/28

POOR GIRL..WE WERE FLYING OVER PARIS AND SHE FELL OUT OF THE PLANE..

FORTUNATELY, WE WERE FLYING VERY LOW

YOU SHOULD DO SOMETHING ABOUT THAT DOG, CHUCK..
SCHULZ

CIVILIANS SHOULDN'T BE ALLOWED ON THE AËRODROME..

PEANUTS
by
SCHULZ

8-29
SCHULZ

I'VE ALWAYS WONDERED WHY BIRDS FLY IN A "V" FORMATION...

8-30
YOUR MOM TOLD YOU TO?
SCHULZ

"'WHAT A CURIOUS FEELING,' SAID ALICE"

"SHE WAS NOW ONLY TEN INCHES HIGH.."

"NOW SHE WAS MORE THAN NINE FEET HIGH..."

"'HOW CAN I HAVE DONE THIS?' SHE THOUGHT."
8-31

"'I MUST BE GETTING SMALL AGAIN.'"
RIGHT
SCHULZ

SCHOOL STARTS NEXT WEEK.. I NEED YOU TO TEST ME ON MY MULTIPLICATION TABLES...

OKAY, HOW MUCH IS FIVE TIMES EIGHT?

WHO CARES?
I THINK YOU'RE READY
SCHULZ
9-1

TOO BIG FOR YOU? ALL RIGHT, BRING YOUR OWN BALL..
9-2

WHAT HAPPENS IF I SWALLOW IT ?
SCHULZ

9-3

WHEE!

IT'S HARD TO EXPLAIN WHY BALLOONS ARE SO MUCH FUN
SCHULZ

HI! I GUESS YOU KNOW THAT SCHOOL STARTS NEXT WEEK..

BEFORE YOU KNOW IT THOUSANDS OF SCREAMING KIDS WILL BE RUNNING THROUGH YOUR HALLS!
9-4

JUST THINKING ABOUT IT GIVES ME ROOM-ACHE!
SCHULZ

CLUMP CLOMP CLUMP CLUMP
PEANUTS®
by SCHULZ

HEY! YOU GOT SHOES!
9-5

THEY LOOK GREAT... YOU GOT SHOES JUST LIKE MICKEY MOUSE!

BUT LET ME ASK YOU SOMETHING...

WHAT DO YOU THINK OTHER BIRDS ARE GOING TO SAY? WHAT IF THEY TEASE YOU?

WHAT IF THEY SAY STUPID THINGS TO YOU LIKE, "DOES YOUR MOTHER WEAR ARMY BOOTS?"

WHICH LEADS ME TO ASK YOU SOMETHING ELSE..

DOES YOUR MOTHER WEAR ARMY BOOTS?

HAHAHA

THUMP!

I WONDER IF MICKEY'S MOM WORE ARMY BOOTS..
SCHULZ

SCHOOL STARTS TOMORROW!!
9-6

WOULD YOU RECOGNIZE THE PRINCIPAL IF YOU MET HIM ON THE STREET ?! BE READY! BE READY!
SCHULZ

AFTER I GRADUATE FROM SCHOOL, WILL I BE A BETTER PERSON?
PROBABLY.. A GOOD EDUCATION IS VERY IMPORTANT
THAT'S RIGHT.. LEARNING ALWAYS MAKES YOU A BETTER PERSON..
UNLESS YOU DON'T HAVE A DOG..
9-7
SCHULZ

9-8
Z

YES, MA'AM.. I'M AWAKE!

DO I HAVE ANYTHING TO TELL THE CLASS? YES, MA'AM..
SCHULZ

THERE'S A SPIDER ON THE CEILING..

HEY, MARCIE, WE DON'T HAVE ANY HOMEWORK TONIGHT, DO WE? WE **DO**?!

PAGE SIXTEEN? PAGE SIXTEEN OF WHAT?

A BOOK? WHAT BOOK?
9-9

DON'T HANG UP, MARCIE..
SCHULZ

SORRY, MA'AM..I WASN'T LISTENING..I WAS THINKING ABOUT MY DOG...

HE ALWAYS WAITS FOR ME TO COME HOME.. NO, HE DOESN'T WAIT FOR ME AT THE GATE..
9-10

WE DON'T HAVE A GATE..

IT'S EMBARRASSING TO WAIT FOR SOMEONE WHEN YOU DON'T HAVE A GATE..
SCHULZ

HERE, I NEED YOU TO TEST ME ON THESE HISTORICAL DATES..

IN WHAT YEAR DID THE VISIGOTHS CROSS THE DANUBE?
9-11

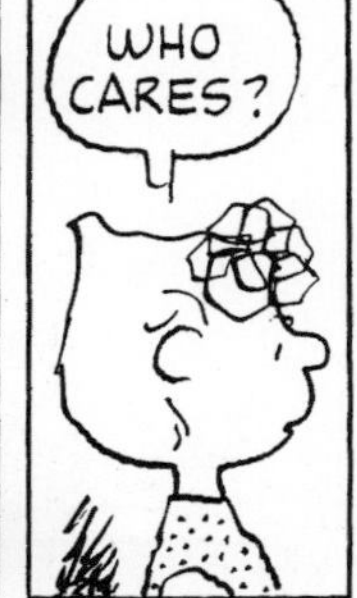
WHO CARES?

I'VE ALWAYS BEEN GOOD WITH HISTORICAL DATES..
SCHULZ

PEANUTS
by SCHULZ

YOU'LL PRAY FOR ME? WHY? I'LL PRAY FOR MYSELF!

"CALL NOW FOR BEST SEATS"... BEST SEATS FOR WHAT?

"STAY TUNED FOR THE WEATHER AND TRAFFIC REPORT!" WHAT DO THEY MEAN, STAY TUNED?

I WASN'T EVEN LISTENING! WHAT DO I NEED A TRAFFIC REPORT FOR? I DON'T HAVE A CAR!

TEN DOLLARS?! THEY WANT ME TO SEND TEN DOLLARS FOR A TAPE OF THEIR PROGRAM? I DIDN'T EVEN LIKE THEIR PROGRAM!
9-12

AND LOOK THERE! HE WANTS ME TO SEND HIM FIFTY DOLLARS SO HE WON'T GO OFF THE AIR! WHAT DO I CARE IF HE GOES OFF? ALL HE DOES IS TALK!

THERE! NOW YOU DON'T HAVE TO DO ANY OF THOSE THINGS..
CLICK!

WHEW! WHAT A RELIEF! THANK YOU, BIG BROTHER..

YOU SHOULD HAVE BEEN AN ATTORNEY
SCHULZ

BING ♫
♫ BONG

9-13

FOOTBALL TIME AGAIN, CHUCK!
SCHULZ

GO STRAIGHT DOWN THE FIELD, MARCIE, CUT LEFT, AND I'LL HIT YOU..

9-14

HIT ME WITH WHAT ?
SCHULZ

I'LL RUN DOWN THE FIELD, MARCIE, AND YOU THROW ME THE BALL..

9-15

?

MARCIE! WHERE DID YOU GO?!

AFTER YOU RAN DOWN THE FIELD, I SUDDENLY FELT VERY LONELY..
SCHULZ

ARE YOU READY?
9-16

I'M READY, MARCIE, BUT BEFORE YOU KICK THE BALL, SQUEEZE IT A FEW TIMES...

WHAT IF IT BECOMES FOND OF ME?
SCHULZ

MY DAD BOUGHT ME THIS HELMET, SIR.. HE SAYS GIRLS CAN PLAY SPORTS JUST AS WELL AS BOYS CAN..
9-17

I TRIED IT IN THE POOL, AND I ALMOST DROWNED..
SCHULZ

9-18

YOU THINK YOU'RE VERY CLEVER, DON'T YOU?
SCHULZ

PEANUTS
by SCHULZ

SUPPERTIME!

SUPPERTIME?

YEAHH! IT'S SUPPERTIME!!

HERE WE GO AGAIN..ALL THAT DANCING AROUND..

SUPPERTIME!
9-19

SUPP..SUPP..SUPPERTIME!

AND THEN HE ALWAYS EXPECTS ME TO JOIN IN..

..AND I'VE NEVER LEARNED THE TEXAS TWO-STEP
SLOW, SLOW, QUICK, QUICK!
SCHULZ

SCHOOL STARTED LAST WEEK!!

9-20
I WASN'T SURE YOU HAD NOTICED
SCHULZ

MY DAD TOOK ME TO MY FIRST HOCKEY GAME LAST NIGHT..

IT WAS REALLY GREAT..

I LOVED WATCHING THE ZAMBONI GO AROUND..
YOU'RE VERY WEIRD, MARCIE..
SCHULZ
9-21

GRAMMA SAYS THAT JUST BEFORE SHE GOES TO SLEEP EACH NIGHT, SHE HEARS ANGELS SINGING..

I HEARD SOMETHING LIKE THAT MYSELF LAST NIGHT...

YOU HEARD ANGELS SINGING?
NO, MY DOG WANTED TO COME IN..
SCHULZ
9-22

I CAN'T REMEMBER MY LOCKER COMBINATION
9-23

WE DON'T HAVE LOCKERS IN OUR SCHOOL..
U.S. MAIL

THAT WAS ANOTHER THING I COULDN'T REMEMBER
SCHULZ

I KNOW YOU'RE THINKING OF GRABBING THIS BLANKET, AND DRAGGING ME ALL OVER THE NEIGHBORHOOD

THEREFORE, I WOULD SUGGEST YOU PUT THAT THOUGHT IN THE DEEPEST RECESS OF YOUR MIND..

9-24

DOGS' MINDS DON'T HAVE RECESSES!
SCHULZ

FINESSE!
9-25
SCHULZ

PEANUTS®
by SCHULZ

AND THEN I WAS WONDERING WHY PEOPLE BECOME ATTORNEYS..
THAT'S WHERE THE COOKIES ARE..

I HEAR WE'RE NOT SUPPOSED TO JOKE ABOUT ATTORNEYS ANYMORE..

WHY IS THIS?

IS IT BECAUSE YOU'RE MORE SENSITIVE THAN YOU USED TO BE?

HEY! GET A LOAD OF THE FUNNY LOOKING ATTORNEY! HE'S DRESSED IN A DOG SUIT!

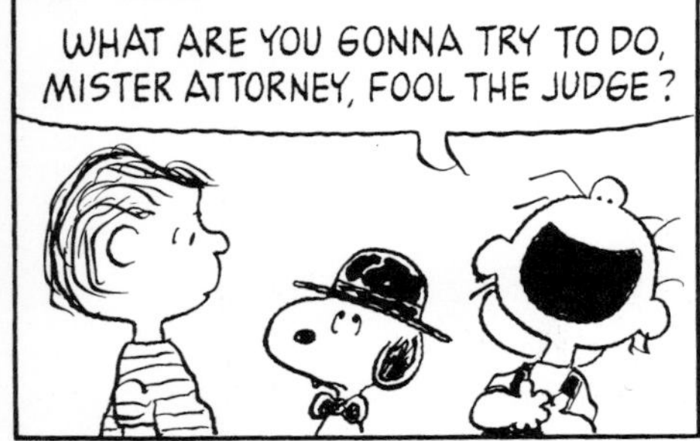
WHAT ARE YOU GONNA TRY TO DO, MISTER ATTORNEY, FOOL THE JUDGE?

9-26
WHAP!!

I GUESS YOU ARE SENSITIVE, AREN'T YOU?
ATTORNEYS ARE BORN SENSITIVE
SCHULZ

MY DAD TOOK ME TO ANOTHER HOCKEY GAME LAST NIGHT..

I GOT TO MEET THE MAN WHO DRIVES THE ZUCCHINI..

ZAMBONI..

9-27
WHATEVER
SCHULZ

I'M AWAKE!
9-28

BUT I CAN'T GET DRESSED RIGHT AWAY..

SCHULZ
MY SOCKS ARE STILL SLEEPING

9-29
Z
Z
Z
Z
Z
U.S. MAIL
WHY DO I HAVE THE FEELING THE SCHOOL BUS HAS BROKEN DOWN AGAIN?
SCHULZ

I THINK I'LL ASK THE TEACHER IF I CAN MOVE MY DESK NEXT TO THAT LITTLE RED-HAIRED GIRL..
9-30

THEN, ONE DAY I CAN REACH OVER AND TOUCH HER HAND..

AND SHE CAN LOOK AT ME LIKE I'VE LOST MY MIND!

MAYBE I'LL ASK THE TEACHER IF I CAN MOVE MY DESK OUT INTO THE HALLWAY..
SCHULZ

OKAY, MARCIE, WHEN I COME RUNNING DOWN THE FIELD, YOU TRY TO STOP ME..

AND DON'T FORGET TO USE YOUR HELMET..
10-1

BONK!

THANKS FOR THE SUGGESTION, SIR!
SCHULZ

YOU DIDN'T KNOW THAT THE EARTH ROTATES?

WELL, I SUPPOSE THERE ARE A LOT OF THINGS YOU DON'T HAVE TO KNOW IF YOU'RE A BIRD..

LIFE IS MORE DIFFICULT FOR DOGS.. WE'RE REQUIRED TO KNOW EVERYTHING

?
YES, MOST OF US REMAIN QUITE HUMBLE..
SCHULZ
10-2

PEANUTS
by SCHULZ

OVER HERE!

THIS IS A BRAND NEW BALL, CHARLIE BROWN! I'LL HOLD IT, AND YOU COME RUNNING UP, AND KICK IT!

A BRAND NEW BALL! WOW!

THIS IS A REAL TREAT!
10-3

AAUGH!

WUMP

IT SUDDENLY OCCURRED TO ME THAT IF I LET YOU KICK IT, IT WOULDN'T BE NEW ANYMORE..
SCHULZ

10-4

PLEASE, YOU DON'T HAVE TO TELL ME EVERY LITTLE DETAIL!
SCHULZ

YES, MA'AM.. THE ANSWER IS "TWELVE"

IT IS? I WAS RIGHT?
10-5

TAKE IT EASY, MA'AM..

SPLASH A LITTLE COLD WATER ON YOUR FACE, AND YOU'LL FEEL BETTER..
SCHULZ

IF YOU REALLY LOVED ME, YOU'D BUY ME A MUSIC BOX..

IF YOU REALLY LOVED **ME**, YOU WOULDN'T ASK ME TO BUY YOU A MUSIC BOX..
10-6

ANOTHER TIE
SCHULZ

I THINK A MUSIC BOX IS THE MOST ROMANTIC GIFT THAT A BOY CAN GIVE TO A GIRL..

HOW ABOUT HALF OF A PEANUT BUTTER SANDWICH?

10-7
WHAT SONG DOES IT PLAY?

A MUSIC BOX! LINUS, YOU BOUGHT ME A MUSIC BOX!

WELL, YOU SAID A MUSIC BOX IS THE MOST ROMANTIC GIFT THAT A BOY CAN GIVE TO A GIRL..
10-8

IT IS! IT'S VERY SPECIAL..

I'LL PUT IT WITH ALL THE OTHERS

10-9

OKAY, GO LEAN ON A CAT!

PEANUTS
by SCHULZ

YES, MA'AM..I'M READY...

THIS IS MY REPORT ON AUTUMN..

WHEN AUTUMN COMES, THE LEAVES BEGIN TO FALL...

NOW, I NEED A VOLUNTEER FROM THE CLASS..HOW ABOUT YOU? THE STUPID LOOKING KID IN THE FRONT ROW..

ALL RIGHT, LET'S SAY THIS KID IS WALKING THROUGH THE WOODS..

SUDDENLY, THE LEAVES BEGIN TO FALL..
10-10

IT'S AUTUMN !!

THANKS, KID! YOU WERE GREAT! JUST STAY AWAY FROM ANYONE WHO HAS A RAKE..
SCHULZ

I NEED YOU TO WRITE A THEME FOR ME..

IF YOU DON'T WRITE IT YOURSELF, HOW WILL YOU EVER LEARN?

10-11
LEARN?
SCHULZ

Dear Brother Snoopy,
Life here on the desert is exciting.
10-12

Last night the sun went down and this morning the sun came up.

There's always something happening.
SCHULZ

IF EVERYONE LISTENED TO ME, THIS WOULD BE A PERFECT WORLD!

JUST THINK ABOUT IT..WOULDN'T YOU LOVE TO LIVE IN A PERFECT WORLD?

10-13

WELL, WHY NOT?!
SCHULZ

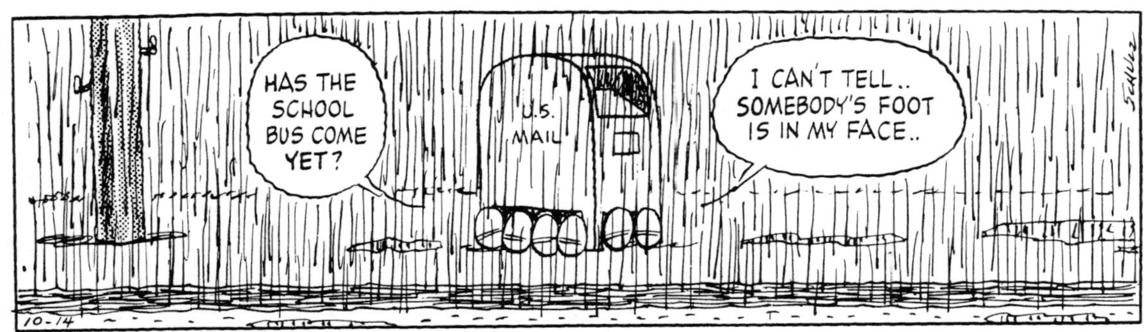
HAS THE SCHOOL BUS COME YET?
U.S. MAIL
I CAN'T TELL.. SOMEBODY'S FOOT IS IN MY FACE..
SCHULZ
10-14

Z

AFRICA! SIXTEEN! SHAKESPEARE! ALABAMA! THE RIVER NILE!
10-15

WERE ANY OF THOSE RIGHT, MA'AM? I COULD TELL HER WHEN SHE WAKES UP AGAIN..
Z
SCHULZ

I'M READY, SIR..

LET'S GO OUT AND KICK THAT BALL AROUND ON THE OL' GRIDLOCK!

GRIDIRON, MARCIE..
WHATEVER
SCHULZ
10-16

PEANUTS
by SCHULZ

LUNCH TIME, SIR..
GOOD!

MOVE OVER, LITTLE GIRLS..LET A MAN SIT DOWN!

GIRLS TAKE UP TOO MUCH ROOM.. GIRLS ARE ALWAYS IN THE WAY...

MIRIAM WAS MOSES' OLDER SISTER.. IN CHAPTER TWELVE OF THE BOOK OF "NUMBERS" SHE ASKS, "HAS THE LORD SPOKEN ONLY THROUGH MOSES?"

WHAT'S THAT SUPPOSED TO MEAN?

I'LL EXPLAIN IT TO HIM, MARCIE...

POW!
10-17

HAM AND CHEESE TODAY, SIR..
PEANUT BUTTER AGAIN, MARCIE
MOSES? WHO WAS MOSES?
SCHULZ

SOMEDAY I WANT TO GO OVER TO JERICHO, AND WATCH THE WALLS COME TUMBLING DOWN

I THINK YOU'RE ABOUT THREE THOUSAND YEARS TOO LATE..

RATS! NOBODY EVER TELLS ME ANYTHING!
10-18
SCHULZ

NOTHING IS MORE EMPTY THAN AN EMPTY MAILBOX..
10-19

IF YOU PUT YOUR EAR UP REAL CLOSE, YOU CAN HEAR THE OCEAN ROAR..
SCHULZ

I THINK SOUNDS ARE INTERESTING, DON'T YOU?
10-20

WHAT IS YOUR FAVORITE SOUND?

KLUNK

"KLUNK"? YES, "KLUNK" IS A VERY INTERESTING SOUND..
SCHULZ

SIR, INSTEAD OF PLAYING, MAYBE I SHOULD JUST BE A CHEERLEADER..
10-21

LISTEN TO THIS...

COME ON, TEAM! TRY TO DO YOUR VERY BEST!!

A LITTLE TOO IMPASSIONED, HUH?
LET'S JUST WORK ON SOME MORE PLAYS, MARCIE
SCHULZ

"FIGHT, FIGHT, FIGHT WITH ALL YOUR MIGHT, AND GO ON TO A HIGHER HEIGHT!"

MARCIE, THAT'S THE WORST CHEER I'VE EVER HEARD!
I HAD HOPED IT WOULD BE INSPIRATIONAL, SIR..
10-22

IT'LL INSPIRE EVERYONE TO GO HOME..
HOW ABOUT, "TURN OUT THE LIGHTS, LUNCH IS OVER"?
SCHULZ

HEY, CHUCK.. I WAS WONDERING IF YOU NEED A CHEERLEADER FOR YOUR FOOTBALL TEAM..

STUPID MARCIE HERE THINKS SHE CAN BE A CHEERLEADER..

SORRY, I ALREADY HAVE ONE..
"WOOF WOOF! ARF ARF! LET'S GET 'EM IN THE SECOND HARF!"
SCHULZ
10-23

PEANUTS
by SCHULZ
EDITORIAL QUEEN

It was a dark and stormy night

Suddenly, a shot rang out.
10-24

LET ME SEE WHAT YOU'VE WRITTEN SO FAR..

YOU KNOW, WHEN YOU'RE WRITING A STORY, IT'S VERY IMPORTANT TO SELECT THE PERFECT WORDS...

IN THIS CASE, I WONDER IF "SUDDENLY" IS THE RIGHT WORD..

Gradually, a shot rang out.
SCHULZ

THIS GAME IS GOING INTO OVERTIME..
IT MUST BE MIDNIGHT WHERE THEY'RE PLAYING..
I'M SURPRISED THE CROWD IS STILL THERE..
THEY SHOULD GO HOME AND FEED THEIR DOG..

I GOT A "C," AN "A," AN "R" AND A "D"! ..NOT TOO BAD, HUH, MARCIE?

THAT'S "CARD," SIR... IT SAYS "REPORT CARD"

I WAS WONDERING HOW I GOT AN "R"...

THE LOCH NESS PUTTER!

WHERE ARE YOU GOING?
OUT TO MAKE MONEY RAKING LEAVES..
10-28

I'M GOING TO USE SALESMANSHIP..I'LL CONVINCE EVERYONE THEY NEED THEIR LEAVES RAKED!

IT'S ALL A MATTER OF SALESMANSHIP, PERSEVERANCE AND BEING WELL LIKED..

WILLY LOMAN OF THE LEAVES
SCHULZ

ASK YOUR DAD IF HE WANTS ME TO RAKE YOUR LEAVES..

10-29

HE SAYS, "HOW MUCH FOR JUST ONE LEAF?"
SCHULZ

MY DAD THINKS HE'S VERY FUNNY

HOW DID IT GO? DID YOU MAKE ANY MONEY DOING LEAVES?
NO, NOT A PENNY..

MAYBE I CAN TRY IT..COULD I BORROW YOUR CLUB?
RAKE

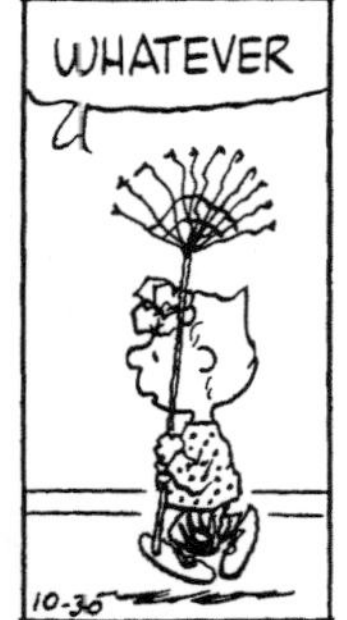
WHATEVER
10-30

OKAY, HERE'S HOW IT WORKS..I RENT YOU THE RAKE, SEE, AND..
SCHULZ

PEANUTS
by
SCHULZ

NOW WHAT?

EXPLAIN TO ME WHAT I'M DOING OUT HERE..
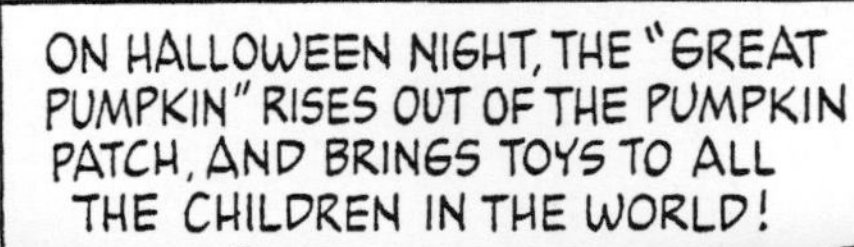
ON HALLOWEEN NIGHT, THE "GREAT PUMPKIN" RISES OUT OF THE PUMPKIN PATCH, AND BRINGS TOYS TO ALL THE CHILDREN IN THE WORLD!

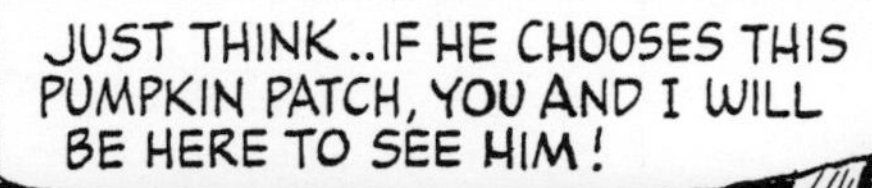
JUST THINK..IF HE CHOOSES THIS PUMPKIN PATCH, YOU AND I WILL BE HERE TO SEE HIM!

10-31

LOOK! THERE HE IS! IT'S THE "GREAT PUMPKIN"!

THAT'S NOT THE "GREAT PUMPKIN"... THAT'S A DOG HOLDING A PUMPKIN ON A STICK!

EXPLAIN TO ME AGAIN WHAT I'M DOING OUT HERE..
TRICK OR TREAT!
SCHULZ

HERE'S THE WORLD WAR I FLYING ACE SITTING IN A SMALL FRENCH CAFE.. THE WAR DRAGS ON... HE IS DEPRESSED..

CHARLES, YOUR DOG IS IN OUR KITCHEN AGAIN DRINKING ALL OUR ROOT BEER..
11-1

GENERAL PERSHING SAYS FOR YOU TO GET BACK TO THE AERODROME RIGHT AWAY..

PRESSURE AGAIN FROM HEADQUARTERS, RAIN AND MUD,... DESPAIR...

MOM!

HERE'S THE WORLD WAR I FLYING ACE WALKING BACK TO THE AERODROME..

SUDDENLY HE SEES A LIGHT IN THE WINDOW OF A SMALL SHABBY FARM HOUSE
11-2

HE TAPS GENTLY ON THE DOOR..
BAM! BAM! BAM!!

GO ON HOME, YOU STUPID BEAGLE!

SOMETIMES THE UNIFORM FRIGHTENS THEM..

BEFORE HE GETS BACK TO THE AERODROME, THE FLYING ACE FEELS HE NEEDS ONE MORE ROOT BEER..

HE ENTERS ANOTHER SMALL SEEDY CAFE, AND BECKONS TO THE PLAIN LOOKING WAITRESS...

HEY, CHUCK! YOUR DOG JUST WALKED INTO OUR HOUSE..
11/3

WELL, YEAH, HE SEEMED TO WANT SOMETHING TO DRINK..I GAVE HIM WHAT WE HAD...

PRETTY CHEAP ROOT BEER..

OKAY, FLYING ACE.. YOU'VE HAD ENOUGH... YOU'D BETTER GET GOING..

SMAK!

PATHETIC CREATURE..SHE SEEMED RATHER LONELY..
11-4

I WAS PASSING BY THIS QUAINT JOINT, AND HEARD THE TINKLING OF A PIANO..
11-5

PLAY "TIPPERARY" FOR ME, SON..I FEEL SORT OF DOWN TONIGHT...

HI, CHARLES..DID YOUR DOG GET HOME ALL RIGHT?
11-6

SURE, CHARLIE BROWN, HE ALMOST KICKED OUR DOOR DOWN!

HEY, CHUCK, THAT'S A WEIRD DOG YOU'VE GOT THERE!

SO ALL I'M SAYING IS I DON'T WANT HIM LEANING ON MY PIANO..

WHY CAN'T I HAVE A NORMAL DOG LIKE EVERYONE ELSE?
WAS THAT GENERAL PERSHING? TELL HIM I'M ON MY WAY..

PEANUTS
by SCHULZ
AND DON'T FORGET YOUR LUNCH

GRAMPA SAYS HE USED TO WALK TEN MILES TO SCHOOL IN THE DEEP SNOW..

HA! LOOK AT THIS!

WAIT 'TIL I TELL HIM ABOUT TODAY! OH, BOY!

I'LL TELL HIM HOW IT STARTED TO SNOW WHILE WE WERE WAITING FOR THE SCHOOL BUS..

AND SUDDENLY IT TURNED INTO A BLIZZARD, AND THE BUS GOT STUCK IN HUGE SNOW DRIFTS..

AND ALL THE SCHOOLS HAD TO CLOSE, AND..

11-7
RATS!
SCHULZ

IT IS DAWN..
HERE'S THE WORLD WAR I FLYING ACE WALKING ONTO THE AERODROME

11-8

HE CLIMBS INTO THE COCKPIT OF HIS SOPWITH CAMEL, AND ADJUSTS THE SUTTON HARNESS...

NOW, THE EARLY MORNING QUIET IS SHATTERED BY THE ROAR OF THE 110 HP LE RHÔNE ENGINE!

SOME PEOPLE HAVE DOGS WHO BARK A LOT, OR DIG HOLES IN THE GARDEN, OR...
SCHULZ

HERE'S THE WORLD WAR I FLYING ACE SEARCHING THE SKY FOR HIS ENEMY, THE RED BARON..

SUDDENLY, OUT OF NOWHERE, A HAIL OF BULLETS RIPS THE FABRIC OF HIS SOPWITH CAMEL!

WITH UNBELIEVABLE SKILL HE GUIDES THE STRICKEN CRAFT BACK TO THE AERODROME

FEARING A FIERY EXPLOSION, HE LEAPS FROM THE COCKPIT!

WHAT'S A SUPPER DISH DOING ON THE RUNWAY?!
SCHULZ 11-9

WHY DOES YOUR DOG STAND IN THE BACKYARD JUST STARING AT HIS DOGHOUSE?

THAT STUPID RED BARON..LOOK WHAT HE DID TO MY PLANE...
SCHULZ 11-10

ON VETERANS DAY I ALWAYS GO OVER TO BILL MAULDIN'S HOUSE TO QUAFF A FEW ROOT BEERS..

BILL KNEW MY HERO, AUDIE MURPHY..
11-11

I'VE TOLD BILL HOW I MET CAPTAIN HARRY TRUMAN IN FRANCE...

BUT BILL NEVER BELIEVES ME..
SCHULZ

ARE YOU THROUGH WITH THE SPORTS SECTION?
WHY? YOU DON'T KNOW ANYTHING ABOUT SPORTS..

IS THERE AN "ANYTHING" SECTION FOR SOMEONE WHO DOESN'T KNOW ANYTHING ABOUT ANYTHING?
SCHULZ
11-12

SOMETIMES, I LIE AWAKE AT NIGHT, AND I ASK, "WHY ME?"
11-13

THEN A VOICE ANSWERS "NOTHING PERSONAL.. YOUR NAME JUST HAPPENED TO COME UP.."
SCHULZ

PEANUTS
by SCHULZ

11-14

WHAT HAPPENED TO HIM?
I THINK IT'S HAPPENED BEFORE..

HE GETS HYPNOTIZED WATCHING THE ZAMBONI GO AROUND..
SCHULZ

TODAY ?! THE TEST IS TODAY ?
YES, MA'AM, I'M SURPRISED..
11-15

I THOUGHT MAYBE BEFORE THE REAL TEST THERE'D BE A PRO-AM ..
SCHULZ

THIS CAN OF DOG FOOD COST EIGHTY-NINE CENTS..

THIS FROZEN DINNER YOU'RE HAVING TONIGHT COST THREE DOLLARS AND FIFTY CENTS..
11-16

MOM AND DAD SHOULD TRADE YOU IN FOR ANOTHER DOG..

STOP GRINNING
SCHULZ

MY DAD'S TAKING ME TO ANOTHER HOCKEY GAME TONIGHT..
11 17

I THINK WE'RE GOING TO SEE THE "MIGHTY FLAMINGOS"
"DUCKS," MARCIE

SOMETHING LIKE THAT ..
DON'T GET RUN OVER BY THE ZUCCHINI..

ZAMBONI, SIR..
YOU'RE GETTING THERE, MARCIE
SCHULZ

THIS IS MY REPORT ON A REAL HOCKEY PUCK..

I GOT IT LAST NIGHT AT THE GAME WITH THE "MIGHTY FLAMINGOS"
11-18

MY DAD WANTED ME TO GET IT AUTOGRAPHED..

I TOLD HIM I THINK AUTOGRAPHING IS STUPID..

BESIDES, I SAID, YOU WERE THE ONE IT HIT ON THE HEAD!
SCHULZ

DID YOU KNOW IT TOOK LEO TOLSTOY SIX YEARS TO WRITE "WAR AND PEACE"?

I KNOW HOW HE MUST HAVE FELT..
11-19

I'VE BEEN WORKING ON THIS STORY NOW FOR OVER HALF AN HOUR..
SCHULZ

I NEED HELP WITH MY HOMEWORK
WHICH SUBJECT?

SUBJECT?
11-20

YOU MEAN WE HAVE SUBJECTS?
SCHULZ

PEANUTS
by SCHULZ

SUPPERTIME! I'M COMING TO GET YOUR DISH

I CAN NEVER REMEMBER..IS THE RED DISH THE SUPPER DISH OR IS THE YELLOW DISH THE SUPPER DISH?

THERE'S STILL SOME WATER IN THIS YELLOW DISH SO IT WOULD SEEM TO ME THAT THIS IS THE WATER DISH..

OF COURSE, THERE'S STILL SOME WATER IN THE YELLOW DISH SO THAT PROBABLY MEANS IT'S THE WATER DISH...

WHICH MEANS THE RED DISH MUST BE THE SUPPER DISH!

11-21
EVERYTHING HE KNOWS HE'S LEARNED FROM ME..
SCHULZ

I'VE DECIDED TO SPEND THE REST OF MY LIFE LOOKING FOR "THE BIG ROCK CANDY MOUNTAIN"
11-22

I DIDN'T FIND IT TODAY, BUT MAYBE I'LL FIND IT TOMORROW..

IF YOU REALLY WANT SOMETHING IN THIS LIFE, YOU HAVE TO BE DETERMINED!

IF I DON'T FIND IT TOMORROW, I THINK I'LL QUIT LOOKING..
SCHULZ

11-23
HAS THE SCHOOL BUS COME YET?

WHY DON'T YOU OPEN YOUR EYES AND SEE FOR YOURSELF?

IT'S TOO EARLY IN THE MORNING TO GO TO ALL THAT TROUBLE..
SCHULZ

YES, MA'AM, I WALKED TO SCHOOL IN THE RAIN..
11-24

YES, MA'AM.. MY WET HAIR IS DRIPPING ON THE DESK, AND THE WATER SEEMS TO BE RUNNING DOWN THE AISLE...

NO, MA'AM, IT'S THE KIDS BEHIND ME WHO ARE MAKING THE LITTLE PAPER SAILBOATS..
SCHULZ

THIS FOOTBALL LOOKS LIKE A THANKSGIVING TURKEY WITHOUT THE DRUMSTICKS..

CATCH THE TURKEY, SIR! WHITE MEAT OR DARK MEAT? SAVE ME THE WISHBONE!

11-25

THE TURKEY FELL OFF THE TABLE, SIR..

I HATE PLAYING WITH YOU, MARCIE!
SCHULZ

SURE, I CAN COUNT.. I SEE EIGHT FINGERS AND TWO THUMBS...

AND ONE NOSE, AND TWO EYES, AND ONE MOUTH, AND TWO EARS...

11-26
AND ONE BIG SISTER!

IT'S GOING TO BE COLD TONIGHT SO I THOUGHT YOU MIGHT WANT TO USE THIS BEDROLL..
11-27

THOUGHTFUL, BUT SORT OF USELESS..
SCHULZ

PEANUTS
by SCHULZ

11-28

ARE WE THERE?
SCHULZ

I WONDER IF THEY HAVE FRACTIONS IN HEAVEN..

NO FRACTIONS, SIR..NO DECIMALS, EITHER...
HOW ABOUT COMMAS?

THERE HAVE TO BE COMMAS, SIR.. WE CAN'T AVOID THEM
11-29

ETERNITY'S GOING TO BE LONGER THAN I THOUGHT..
SCHULZ

WELL, I'LL BE! THIS IS THE SAME LITTLE BUG I SAW OVER ON THE PLAYGROUND TWO DAYS AGO..

11-30
HOW DO YOU KNOW?

I HAVE A GOOD MEMORY FOR FACES
SCHULZ

CAN YOU SEE THE SCHOOL BUS?
NOT YET

I'VE CHANGED MY MIND..I DON'T THINK I'LL GET ON THE BUS..
WHY NOT?
12-1

MY LUNCH JUST WENT HOME..
SCHULZ

HEY, CHUCK, HOW ABOUT A FOOTBALL GAME TOMORROW?

YOU KNOW, A REGULAR STRAIGHT AHEAD, DOWN IN THE DIRT, IN YOUR FACE, ROCK 'EM, SOCK 'EM, ANYTHING GOES, GOOD OLD FASHIONED FOOTBALL GAME!

IS THE LIBRARY OPEN TOMORROW?
SCHULZ
12-2

OKAY, CHUCK..HEADS OR TAILS...YOU CALL IT..

12-3

TELL YOUR PLAYER TO WAIT 'TIL THE COIN COMES DOWN!
SCHULZ

GET READY, MARCIE.. HERE COMES THE KICKOFF..
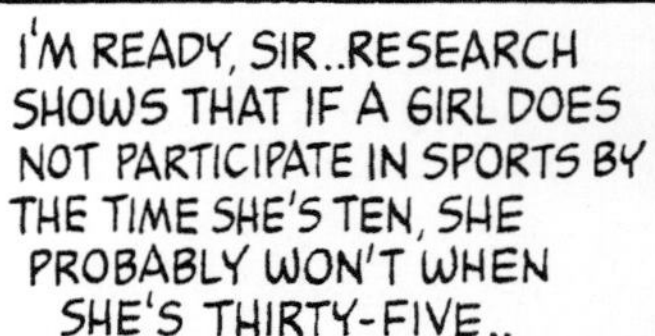
I'M READY, SIR..RESEARCH SHOWS THAT IF A GIRL DOES NOT PARTICIPATE IN SPORTS BY THE TIME SHE'S TEN, SHE PROBABLY WON'T WHEN SHE'S THIRTY-FIVE..

12-4
BONK!

YOU'LL NEVER BE THIRTY-FIVE, MARCIE..
SCHULZ

PEANUTS®
by
SCHULZ

12-5

..SO WHAT WE'RE TALKING ABOUT HERE IS EMPOWERMENT THROUGH INNER DIALOGUE HOPEFULLY LEADING TO LIFE ENHANCEMENT..
SCHULZ

OKAY, FRANKLIN, GO STRAIGHT OUT, THEN CUT RIGHT, AND I'LL HIT YOU WITH THE BOMB..
AREN'T YOU ON THE OTHER TEAM, SWEETIE?
MY GLASSES ARE WET.. I CAN'T SEE A THING..
SCHULZ
12-6

WHERE AM I?
WHO'S GOT THE BALL?
SOMEBODY CALL THE VET!
IS IT STILL RAINING OR AM I BLEEDING?
ISN'T THIS GREAT, CHUCK? GOOD OLD FASHIONED, DOWN IN THE DIRT FOOTBALL!
12-7
SCHULZ

12-8
WE'RE NOT LETTING A LITTLE RAIN SPOIL OUR FUN, ARE WE, CHUCK?
DID SHE SAY "RAIN" OR "PAIN"?
SCHULZ

THANKS FOR THE GAME, CHUCK! I HAD LOTS OF FUN..YOU GUYS HAD FUN, TOO, DIDN'T YOU?
LOTS OF FUN..
FROM NOW ON I'M GOING TO BE A HOUSE DOG..
SCHULZ
12-9

BOY, AFTER A GAME LIKE THAT IT'D BE NICE TO SIT IN A HOT TUB..

I'LL SAY IT WOULD..
12-10

A LOT BETTER THAN A COLD WATER DISH
SCHULZ

WASN'T THAT FUN, MARCIE? GOOD OLD FASHIONED, PLAY IN THE RAIN, DOWN IN THE DIRT, FOOTBALL!
I THINK I LOST MY SHOES..
12-11

AND NOW IT'S STARTING TO SNOW! WE SHOULD PLAY AGAIN TOMORROW..

I NEVER KNEW LIFE COULD BE SO BEAUTIFUL!
SCHULZ

PEANUTS
by SCHULZ
MERCI!

WELL, LOOK HERE! IT'S SANTA! THIS IS MY LITTLE BROTHER "RERUN," SANTA...

TELL SANTA WHAT YOU WANT FOR CHRISTMAS,"RERUN"..

WELL, I'D LIKE SOME BOOKS, A VIDEO GAME, SOME IN-LINE SKATES AND MAYBE A NICE SWEATER..

THAT WAS GREAT,"RERUN"...NOW YOU HAVE SOMETHING TO LOOK FORWARD TO ON CHRISTMAS MORNING..

BEFORE WE GO ANY FARTHER, COULD I ASK YOU SOMETHING?
12-12

DID YOU KNOW I WAS TALKING TO A DOG?
SCHULZ

IF YOU'RE COLLECTING FOR CHARITY, WHAT CHARITY ARE YOU COLLECTING FOR?

12-13
SCHULZ

I HAVE TO READ A BOOK DURING CHRISTMAS VACATION..

TRY THIS ONE.. IT'S A REAL PAGE-TURNER

12-14

I HATE TURNING PAGES
SCHULZ

THIS IS THE BOOK I HAVE TO READ FOR SCHOOL..I WANT YOU TO READ IT FOR ME..
12-15

YOU MEAN I'M SUPPOSED TO READ IT WHILE YOU JUST SIT HERE AND LISTEN..

SCHULZ
LISTEN?

ALL RIGHT, I READ YOUR BOOK FOR YOU... NOW, WHAT DO I DO?

NOW, YOU WRITE THE REPORT..
I HOPE YOU APPRECIATE ALL THIS..

12-16
I'LL SEND YOU A CHRISTMAS CARD
SCHULZ

ALL RIGHT, I WROTE YOUR BOOK REPORT FOR YOU.. SEE WHAT YOU THINK..

"THIS WAS THE MOST EXCITING BOOK I HAVE EVER READ..I LIKED ALL THE CHARACTERS"

"THE DESCRIPTIONS WERE BEAUTIFUL, AND THE STORY VERY SUSPENSEFUL"
12 17

I DON'T KNOW..IF I HAD READ IT, I WOULDN'T HAVE LIKED IT THAT MUCH
SCHULZ

BEND DOWN..
12-18
SCHULZ

PEANUTS®
by SCHULZ

WELL, A BICYCLE WOULD BE NICE..

AND MAYBE A NEW SLED AND A PAIR OF IN-LINE SKATES..

AND MAYBE A JUMP ROPE..

12-19

IT'S NICE TO BE ABLE TO TELL SANTA CLAUS WHAT YOU WANT FOR CHRISTMAS, ISN'T IT?
IF YOU CAN GET PAST THE SECRETARY..
SCHULZ

ONE OF THE GREAT JOYS IN LIFE IS SLIDING ON AN ICY SIDEWALK..

12-20

JOE 'ICE FOLLIES'..
SCHULZ

YES, MA'AM..IT'S COLD OUTSIDE...
12-21

I'D LIKE AN ICE CREAM CONE, PLEASE

DO YOU MIND MITTEN MONEY? THIS IS SOME MONEY THAT'S BEEN IN MY MITTEN SINCE LAST WINTER..

ONE MORE QUESTION..

HOW DO YOU EAT ICE CREAM THROUGH A WOOLEN SCARF?
SCHULZ

WHERE'S MY BIG FURRY HAT?

HAS ANYONE SEEN MY BIG FURRY HAT?
12-22

SCHULZ

I THINK I'VE LEARNED SOMETHING

12-23

YOU CAN SLIDE DOWN THE STEPS..

BUT YOU CAN'T SLIDE..

UP THE STEPS..
SCHULZ

SCHULZ
MERRY CHRISTMAS
12-24

Dear Mom and Dad,
Thank you for the
wonderful present. It
is something I have
always wanted.
12-25
SCHULZ

PEANUTS®
by SCHULZ

WHAT ARE YOU DOING?

I'M WRITING A "THANK YOU" LETTER..WHAT DID I GET FROM GRAMMA FOR CHRISTMAS?

WHICH GRAMMA? YOU'VE GOT TWO OF THEM..

MAYBE I'LL WRITE TO GRAMPA.. WHAT DID I GET FROM GRAMPA?

WHICH GRAMPA? YOU'VE GOT TWO OF 'EM..
12-26

WHAT DID I GET FROM MY AUNT? MAYBE I'LL WRITE TO MY AUNT...

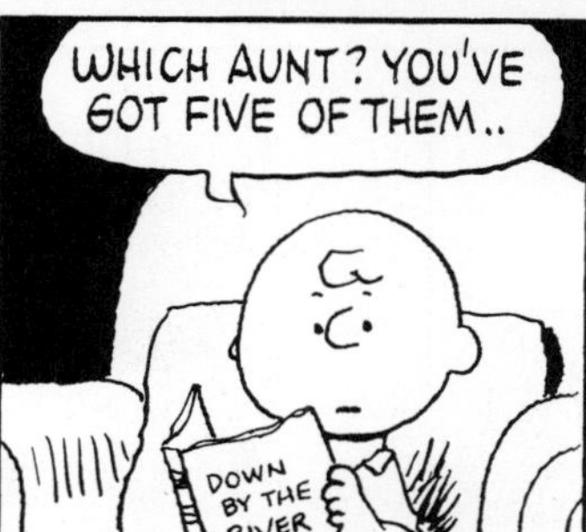
WHICH AUNT? YOU'VE GOT FIVE OF THEM..
DOWN BY THE RIVER

WHAT DID I GET FROM MY THIRD COUSIN ONCE-REMOVED?
SCHULZ

WOULD YOU BE OFFENDED IF I EXCHANGED THE PRESENT YOU GAVE ME FOR CHRISTMAS?
12-27

I DIDN'T GIVE YOU A PRESENT FOR CHRISTMAS..

AND DON'T THINK I DIDN'T NOTICE!
SCHULZ

The Dog-That Most Magnificent of All Creatures.
12-28

WHAT KIND OF DOG ARE YOU TALKING ABOUT?

Any Dog
SCHULZ

I'VE ALWAYS WONDERED HOW THE ZAMBONI GOT OFF THE ICE..
12-29
SCHULZ

" DR. MORTIMER'S VOICE SANK ALMOST TO A WHISPER, AND HE SAID, 'MR.HOLMES, THEY WERE THE FOOTPRINTS OF A GIGANTIC HOUND!'"

WELL, THAT'S ENOUGH READING FOR TONIGHT..
12/30

AND I NEVER SLEEP AGAIN FOR THE REST OF MY LIFE..
SCHULZ

SHALL WE READ SOME MORE OF "THE HOUND OF THE BASKERVILLES" TONIGHT ?
12-31

OKAY, I'M READY..
SCHULZ

The New Year had finally come.
1-1-94

In spite of all that had happened, he knew he had much to be thankful for.

He was still a dog.
SCHULZ

PEANUTS
by
SCHULZ

WOW!

YES, MA'AM..WHAT YOU JUST TOLD US ABOUT THE STARS AND THE PLANETS IS REALLY FASCINATING..

AND YOU KNOW WHO'S INTERESTED IN THIS SORT OF THING?
1-2-94

MY DOG! YES, HE REALLY IS!

SO WHAT I'D LIKE TO DO RIGHT NOW IS RUN HOME, AND TELL HIM ALL ABOUT WHAT YOU JUST TAUGHT US...

YES, MA'AM..

NICE TRY, CHARLIE BROWN
SCHULZ

DID YOU MISS ME DURING CHRISTMAS VACATION?

DID YOU GIVE ME A CHRISTMAS PRESENT?
NO
1-3-94

I DIDN'T MISS YOU
SCHULZ

SCHULZ 1-4-94
AFTER THAT, HOW LONG WAS IT BEFORE YOU SAW YOUR GRANDFATHER AGAIN?

LOOK HERE.. THERE'S A TINY LITTLE BOOK ON THE BOTTOM OF THE BIRD CAGE...

IT'S A DIARY! YOUR GRANDFATHER KEPT A DIARY WHILE HE WAS IN THE CAGE!

"I'VE BEEN IN HERE FOR SIX WEEKS NOW, AND MY ATTORNEY HAS NEVER CALLED BACK.."
1-5-94

YOUR GRANDFATHER WAS AMAZING..HE KEPT A DIARY ALL THE TIME HE WAS IN THE BIRD CAGE...
1-6-94

"MONDAY: I HATE IT IN HERE!"
"TUESDAY: I HATE IT IN HERE!"
"WEDNESDAY: I HATE IT IN HERE!"

NO, I DON'T THINK HE LIKED IT IN THERE..
SCHULZ

YOUR GRAMPA WROTE A LOT IN HIS DIARY..

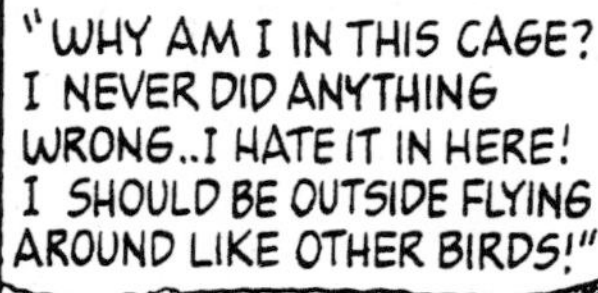

"WHY AM I IN THIS CAGE? I NEVER DID ANYTHING WRONG..I HATE IT IN HERE! I SHOULD BE OUTSIDE FLYING AROUND LIKE OTHER BIRDS!"

"ONCE A WEEK, THEY PUT MY CAGE OUTSIDE IN THE SUN..SOONER OR LATER THEY'RE GOING TO LEAVE THAT LITTLE DOOR OPEN.."

"ANYWAY, THIS IS A STUPID LIFE SITTING HERE ALONE WAITING FOR THAT TO.."
1-8-94

AND THAT'S IT! THE DIARY ENDS RIGHT THERE!

HE PROBABLY GOT OUT, AND IS SITTING ON A TELEPHONE WIRE RIGHT NOW LOOKING DOWN AT US...

EVERY TIME YOU SEE A BIRD SITTING ON A TELEPHONE WIRE, YOU SHOULD WAVE..IT MIGHT BE YOUR GRAMPA!
SCHULZ

PEANUTS
by SCHULZ

1-9

BOOT!

YOU DID WHAT?

WELL, IT COULD BE A MISDEMEANOR OR A FELONY..

KLUNK!

BUT MOST LIKELY IT COULD BE CONSIDERED MAYHEM

KLUNK!

MAYHEM IS "DEPRIVING A HUMAN BEING OF A MEMBER OF HIS BODY.." IN THIS CASE, HIS HEAD, RIGHT ?

NOW, A SNOWMAN ISN'T A HUMAN BEING SO I THINK WE..
KLUNK!

HOW CAN YOU TALK TO A CLIENT WHO KEEPS FAINTING ALL THE TIME ?
SCHULZ

"ALL'S RIGHT WITH THE WORLD"

WHAT DO PEOPLE MEAN WHEN THEY SAY, "ALL'S RIGHT WITH THE WORLD"?
1-10

LUCY'S HERE
SCHULZ

THAT ZAMBONI MAKES GOOD ICE..
SCHULZ
1-11

I HAVE TO DO A BOOK REPORT ON ZECHARIAH
GOOD FOR YOU..

IN A UNIQUE WAY, ZECHARIAH IS ONE OF THE MOST IMPORTANT BOOKS IN THE OLD TESTAMENT..

IF YOU NEED ANY HELP, JUST LET ME KNOW

1-12
HOW DO YOU SPELL IT?
SCHULZ

WHEN I LEFT FOR SCHOOL THIS MORNING, YOU WERE ASLEEP..

WHEN I CAME HOME, YOU WERE STILL ASLEEP..

I FIND THAT INTERESTING, DON'T YOU?
1-13

I CAN'T HEAR YOU..I'M ASLEEP..
SCHULZ

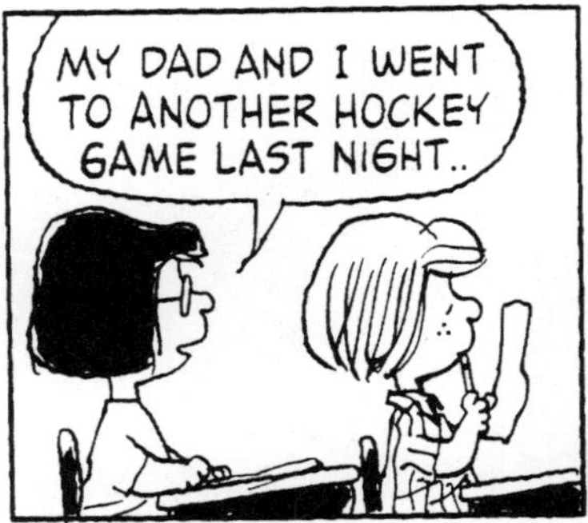
MY DAD AND I WENT TO ANOTHER HOCKEY GAME LAST NIGHT..

IT'S AMAZING HOW FAST THE PLAYERS SKATE UP AND DOWN THE COURT..
RINK

NEXT WEEK WE'RE GOING TO A BASKETBALL RINK
1/14
SCHULZ

"IF YOU GIVE A MOUSE A COOKIE"

YOU SHOULD WRITE A BOOK LIKE THAT..
1-15

"If You Give a Beagle a Brownie"
SCHULZ

PEANUTS
by SCHULZ
"PETANQUE"?

BONJOUR, CAPITAINE!

DOES THE WORLD WAR I FLYING ACE KNOW HOW TO PLAY "PETANQUE"? THEN, I SHALL SHOW HIM..

"PETANQUE" ORIGINATED IN PROVENCE IN 1910..

WE BEGIN BY TOSSING A SMALL WOODEN BALL AHEAD OF US CALLED THE "COCHONNET"

YOU WILL THEN PITCH THIS HEAVY METAL "BOULE" AS CLOSE TO THE "COCHONNET" AS YOU CAN..

OF COURSE, YOU MUST BE CAREFUL NOT TO DROP THE HEAVY "BOULE" ON YOUR..

YIPE!

THE FLYING ACE IS RETURNED TO THE FIELD HOSPITAL..
?
1-16

"WHAT DID YOU DO IN THE GREAT WAR, GRAMPA?" "I WAS WOUNDED PLAYING 'PETANQUE'"
SCHULZ

HOW DO I LOOK? I'M GOING DOWN TO HAVE MY PICTURE TAKEN WITH SANTA CLAUS..

I THINK YOU'RE EITHER ABOUT THREE WEEKS TOO LATE OR MAYBE ELEVEN MONTHS TOO EARLY..
1-17

I'LL GO NOW, AND BE THE FIRST ONE IN LINE
SCHULZ

SCHULZ
ON THE OTHER HAND, MAYBE I SHOULD GO GET MY CAMERA
1-18

OH, NO! I LEFT MY LUNCH ON THE CURB..
1-19

DO YOU THINK THE BUS DRIVER WOULD TURN AROUND AND GO BACK SO I COULD GET IT?

MAYBE, IF YOU ASKED HIM NICELY..

HEY, MAC!
SCHULZ

WHEN PEOPLE WALK BY, AND LOOK IN OUR YARD, I THINK THEY SHOULD SEE A HAPPY DOG..
1-20

RIGHT NOW, NOBODY'S LOOKING...

YOU CAN PUT AWAY THE TAMBOURINE..
SCHULZ

IT SAYS HERE THAT THE AVERAGE CHILD WEARS DOWN 730 CRAYONS BEFORE HE OR SHE IS TEN YEARS OLD..
AND THAT COLORING PROMOTES UNDERSTANDING, AND BRINGS CHILDREN CLOSER TOGETHER..
WHAT COLOR SHOULD I MAKE THE SKY?
BLUE, YOU BLOCKHEAD!
SCHULZ
1-21

I'VE DEVELOPED A NEW IMPROVED PHILOSOPHY..

"WHO CARES? HOW SHOULD I KNOW? DO YOU THINK I'M OUT OF MY MIND?"

A GOOD PHILOSOPHY HELPS YOU ENDURE ALL OF THE TROUBLES WE HAVE IN LIFE..
1-22

"WHO CARES? HOW SHOULD I KNOW? DO YOU THINK I'M OUT OUT OF MY MIND?"
SCHULZ

PEANUTS
by SCHULZ
SORRY

NO MORE SLIDING DOWNHILL IN A CARDBOARD BOX..

NOW I HAVE A REAL SLED!

THE FASTEST SLED IN THE WORLD!
1-23

NOBODY WILL BE ABLE TO BEAT ME!

NOBODY!

SCHULZ

OH, I SEE.. IT WAS A TRICK QUESTION, WASN'T IT?

NO WONDER I GOT IT WRONG..
1-24

CONGRATULATIONS, MA'AM.. YOU DID IT AGAIN!
SCHULZ

THE RAIN IS GETTING MY HOMEWORK ALL WET
I DIDN'T KNOW YOU HAD DONE ANY HOMEWORK
SCHULZ

1-25
IF I HAD DONE MY HOMEWORK, THE RAIN WOULD BE GETTING IT ALL WET

I'VE BEEN FEELING SORT OF LONELY LATELY..
YOU NEED SOME NEW FRIENDS, CHARLIE BROWN, OR A GOOD DOG..

I ALREADY HAVE A DOG..
I SAID A GOOD DOG

DON'T WALK SO FAST.. I'M TRYING TO BITE YOUR LEG!
SCHULZ
1-26

1-27
YOU'RE RIGHT.. IT IS A LITTLE MORE WINDY TODAY THAN USUAL..
SCHULZ

"SILVER BLAZE" BY A. CONAN DOYLE

"..THE CURIOUS INCIDENT OF THE DOG IN THE NIGHTTIME." "THE DOG DID NOTHING IN THE NIGHTTIME." "THAT WAS THE CURIOUS INCIDENT," REMARKED SHERLOCK HOLMES...

1-28
MY FAVORITE PART..
SCHULZ

NOTHING WOULD MAKE ME HAPPIER THAN TO SEE YOU THROW THAT STUPID BLANKET AWAY..

1-29

BACKSPIN!
SCHULZ

PEANUTS
by
SCHULZ
EAT

AH! A CUSTOMER!

GOOD EVENING, SIR.. WELCOME TO AN HOUR OF FINE DINING..

I THINK YOU'RE GOING TO BE VERY PLEASED WITH OUR SPECIAL FOOD AND SPECIAL SERVICE..

1-30
OF COURSE, OUR SPECIAL TONIGHT IS DOG FOOD..

I SHALL NOW GO TO THE KITCHEN, AND PERSONALLY PREPARE YOUR SPECIAL MEAL

YOU'RE GOING TO BE GLAD YOU CAME TO SUCH A SPECIAL PLACE..

IF THIS IS SUCH A SPECIAL PLACE, WHY AM I THE ONLY ONE HERE?
SCHULZ

WHEN YOU WRITE LIKE THAT, DO YOU EVER GET INK ON YOUR FINGERS?

WHAT?
1-31

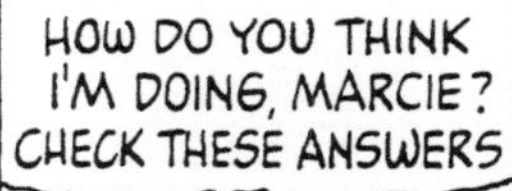
HOW DO YOU THINK I'M DOING, MARCIE? CHECK THESE ANSWERS

YOU GOT THE FIRST NINE QUESTIONS WRONG, SIR..

OH, WELL.. I LEARNED A LONG TIME AGO THAT IT'S NOT HOW YOU START, IT'S HOW YOU FINISH..
2/1

YOU GOT THE LAST ONE WRONG, TOO!

THIS IS MY REPORT ON THE GUY WHO THOUGHT IT UP..

MA'AM?

THE TELEPHONE

ALEXANDER GRAHAM BELL..INVENTED? YES, MA'AM..THE TELEPHONE...

THIS IS MY REPORT ON THE GUY WHO THOUGHT IT UP..
2-2

AND THEN ALEXANDER GRAHAM BELL GOES, "OH, NO!"

AND THEN HE GOES, "MR. WATSON, COME HERE!" AND MR. WATSON GOES, "THAT'S IT!"
2-3

MA'AM?

AND THE TEACHER GOES, "D-MINUS!"
DON'T BUG ME, MARCIE!
SCHULZ

I'VE DECIDED TO TIE A PINK RIBBON AROUND ALL MY LOVE LETTERS..

SEE? I ALREADY HAVE THE RIBBON..

BUT I DON'T HAVE ANY LOVE LETTERS..
SCHULZ
2/4

THERE'S NOTHING MORE PATHETIC THAN A LITTLE DOG SITTING IN THE RAIN..
2-5

THERE'S NOTHING MORE PATHETIC THAN A DOG TOO STUPID TO GET IN OUT OF THE RAIN..

EITHER WAY I'M PATHETIC..
SCHULZ

PEANUTS
by SCHULZ

HOMEMADE VALENTINES
FOR THE ♡ IN YOUR LIFE
I NEED A VALENTINE THAT WILL IMPRESS THIS GIRL I LIKE..

THEN YOU'LL WANT THIS SUPER POTENT VALENTINE!
POTENT?

IT'LL SWEEP HER OFF HER FEET! IT'LL KNOCK HER SOCKS OFF!
ALL RIGHT, I'LL TAKE IT!
FOR THE ♡
2-6

GOOD..IF YOU COME AROUND NEXT FRIDAY, YOU CAN PICK IT UP..
FRIDAY?! WHY CAN'T I HAVE IT NOW?
FOR THE ♡

IT'S TOO POTENT...
FOR THE ♡

THERE'S A FIVE-DAY WAITING PERIOD!
FOR THE ♡ IN YOUR LIFE
SCHULZ

SOMETIMES I LIE AWAKE AT NIGHT, AND I ASK, "WHY AM I HERE?"
2/7

THEN A VOICE ANSWERS, "WHY? WHERE DO YOU WANT TO BE?"
SCHULZ

I GUESS I LEAD KIND OF A SIMPLE LIFE..

BUT YOU KNOW WHAT I NEVER HAVE TO WORRY ABOUT?

2-8
LEAVING MY KEYS IN THE CAR..
SCHULZ

I'M GOING IN TO TOWN TO BUY VALENTINES FOR ALL THE GIRLS WHO LOVE ME..

I SHOULD BE BACK IN TEN SECONDS..
2-9
SCHULZ

I REMEMBER THIS ONE GIRL I WAS IN LOVE WITH A LONG TIME AGO..
2-10

HER FATHER BROKE UP OUR ROMANCE.. HE SAID I'D NEVER AMOUNT TO ANYTHING

BOY, WAS HE WRONG!

WASN'T HE?
SCHULZ

LOOK, I GOT MYSELF A SLEEPING BAG..
2-11

I'M TIRED OF BEING COLD AT NIGHT

I WONDER WHO DESIGNS THESE THINGS..
SCHULZ

ROCK SLIDE AREA
2-12

SCHULZ

PEANUTS®
by
SCHULZ

I AM THE KING!

I AM THE KING OF THE HILL!

NO, YOU'RE NOT!

I AM THE KING OF THE HILL!

2-13

I AM THE KING OF THE HILL!

THE SMALLER THE KING, THE MORE THE TALK..
SCHULZ

BIG BROTHER! WAKE UP! YOUR DOG IS IN THE HOSPITAL!

DAD TOOK HIM IN EARLY THIS MORNING!

YES, MA'AM, HIS NAME IS SNOOPY.. VISITORS? HE ALREADY HAS SOME VISITORS?
2-14

!
SCHULZ

ANDY! SPIKE! OLAF! HOW DID YOU KNOW YOUR BROTHER WAS SICK? HOW DID YOU FIND YOUR WAY HERE?
2-15

ANIMALS HAVE AN INSTINCT ABOUT THINGS LIKE THIS..
WE GO BY INSTINCT
A LOT OF IT WAS LUCK..
SCHULZ

OUR BROTHER SEEMS TO BE SLEEPING ALL RIGHT..
I'VE BEEN THINKING.. DO DOGS GO TO HEAVEN WHEN THEY DIE?
2-16

WHEN THEY WHAT?

WHEN THEY DIE..
I DIDN'T KNOW WE DIE!?
SCHULZ

WAITING ROOM
I HEARD A NURSE SAY OUR BROTHER SNOOPY HAS PNEUMONIA..

HE WAS ALWAYS THE LIVELY ONE IN OUR FAMILY..
2-17

WASN'T HE IN WORLD WAR I?
I THINK HE JUST THOUGHT HE WAS..

YOU KNOW WHAT I ALWAYS WONDERED?
WHERE DID HE GET THE HELMET AND GOGGLES?
SCHULZ

IF WE'RE ALL BROTHERS, HOW COME I'M SO FUZZY, YOU'RE SO SKINNY AND OLAF IS SO FAT?

I'M NOT SKINNY.. I'M TRIM!
AND I'M NOT FAT!

2-18
YOU'RE NOT FAT?
I'M ROLY-POLY!
SCHULZ

I'M GLAD YOU'RE RESTING, SNOOPY.. I'LL BE OUT IN THE WAITING ROOM WITH ANDY AND SPIKE AND OLAF..

BOY, IT TAKES SOMETHING LIKE THIS TO MAKE YOU THINK, DOESN'T IT?
WHEN FISH DIE, DO THEY GO TO HEAVEN?
NOT IF THEY'VE BEEN A BAD FISH
SCHULZ
2-19

PEANUTS®
by SCHULZ
YAWN

Z

2-20

SCHULZ

HOW CAN WE KNOW IF OUR BROTHER IS GETTING BETTER IF NO ONE TELLS US ANYTHING?

2-21

I THINK I'LL GO HANG AROUND THE FRONT DESK.. MAYBE I'LL HEAR SOMETHING...

THE NURSE IS HAVING TROUBLE WITH HER BOYFRIEND, AND THE DOCTOR IS GOING TO SWITCH TO A METAL SEVEN-WOOD!
SCHULZ

MOM? DAD? GUESS WHAT! SNOOPY IS AWAKE, AND HE'S EATING!

YES! HE'S REALLY ENJOYING HIS LUNCH ...IN FACT, THEY ALL ARE!
2-22

SCHULZ

2-23
I CAN'T BELIEVE IT.. YOUR BROTHERS HAVE GONE! THEY KNEW YOU WERE FEELING BETTER SO THEY JUST LEFT...
DOGS DON'T SAY, "GOODBYE"
SCHULZ

2-24

SCHULZ
MY DOG IS HOME!

WHEN YOUR DOG WAS SICK, YOU WERE WORRIED ABOUT HIM, WEREN'T YOU?

IF I GOT SICK, WOULD YOU WORRY THAT MUCH ABOUT ME?
OF COURSE

THAT MUCH, OR MORE?
I CAN'T HEAR YOU..THE TV IS TOO LOUD..

2-25
STUPID DOG!
SCHULZ

YOU'VE TIED YOUR OWN SHOES, RERUN! GOOD FOR YOU

NOW, OF COURSE, THERE'S ONE OTHER THING...
2-26

THE SOCKS GO ON BEFORE THE SHOES..
SCHULZ

PEANUTS
by SCHULZ

THAT'S PERFECT!

WE'LL STAND BY THE DOOR, SEE, AND THEN YOU GO INTO YOUR ACT..

MAYBE WE'LL GET A LITTLE MIDDAY SNACK..

OKAY, GO TO IT..

2-27

DON'T FEEL BAD.. LOTS OF SHOWS CLOSE AFTER ONE PERFORMANCE..
SCHULZ

MARCIE, I DON'T UNDERSTAND THE PROBLEM ON PAGE 362..

THERE IS NO PROBLEM ON PAGE 362, SIR... THAT'S THE INDEX..

PRETTY TRICKY, MA'AM!
SCHULZ
2-28

TELL MY TEACHER TO BRING THE CLASS TO OUR HOUSE TODAY, AND WE CAN STUDY HERE IN MY ROOM..

3-1

SHE SAID IS IT ALL RIGHT TO BRING THE PRINCIPAL, TOO, AND ALL THE MEMBERS OF THE SCHOOL BOARD?

IT WOULD HAVE BEEN PRETTY CROWDED..
SCHULZ

WAKE UP! IT'S A PERFECT DAY FOR CHASING RABBITS!
3-2

WHAT ARE YOU DOING?

YOU DON'T CATCH RABBITS BY HANDING OUT LITERATURE..
SCHULZ

3-3

WAIT HERE.. I'LL GO SEE IF THERE ARE ANY COOKIES LEFT..

NOPE, THE COOKIES ARE ALL GONE..

SO I WASTED A GOOD COOKIE WAIT..
SCHULZ

THIS HAS BEEN A REALLY GOOD DAY..

I DID EVERYTHING RIGHT...
3-4

IN MY OPINION..
SCHULZ

3-5
"DOG FLAKES"? WHO ORDERED "DOG FLAKES"?!
SCHULZ

Dear Diary,
Strange day at school today. I started out feeling perky, and ended up in the wastebasket.

I LOVE THE START OF THE BASEBALL SEASON!

THERE'S A CERTAIN ALMOST INDESCRIBABLE FEELING IN THE AIR..
3-7

DEFEAT!

HOW WOULD YOU LIKE TO BUY THE BAT THAT WAS USED BY ROY HOBBS?
ROY HOBBS WAS A FICTIONAL CHARACTER
3-8

SO IF I SOLD IT TO YOU, IT WOULD BE A REAL CON JOB..
THAT'S RIGHT..

I'LL TRY SOMEBODY ELSE...

HOW WOULD YOU LIKE TO BUY THE BAT THAT WAS USED BY ROY HOBBS?

LOOK WHAT I GOT! THAT WEIRD KID JUST SOLD ME THE BAT THAT WAS USED BY ROY HOBBS!

WHO WAS ROY HOBBS?
WHO WAS ROY HOBBS? ARE YOU KIDDING?
3-9

BOY, LOOK AT THIS BAT! THIS IS A REAL COLLECTOR'S ITEM!

WHO WAS ROY HOBBS?
I DON'T HAVE THE SLIGHTEST IDEA!

HI, CHARLIE BROWN..THIS IS THE WEIRD KID WHO SOLD ME THE BAT USED BY ROY HOBBS..

I ONLY PAID HER A DOLLAR, AND I GOT A REAL COLLECTOR'S ITEM

3-10
ROY HOBBS WAS A FICTIONAL CHARACTER

BE CAREFUL..YOU'RE MESSING UP MY PITCHER'S MOUND!

YOU SOLD ME A WORTHLESS BAT! I DID NOT! I WANT MY DOLLAR BACK! TRY AND GET IT! LET GO OF THAT BAT! LET GO YOURSELF! GIVE ME MY DOLLAR! LET GO! LET GO YOURSELF!!

3-11

CHARLIE BROWN, I WAS GOING TO ASK IF I COULD PLAY ON YOUR TEAM, BUT I'D NEVER WANT TO PLAY ON THE SAME TEAM WITH THIS STUPID GIRL!

OH, YEAH? I'M THE MOST FAITHFUL PLAYER HE HAS!
3-12

FAITHFUL TO WHAT?

THE CATCHER!
I CAN'T STAND IT!

PEANUTS
by SCHULZ
SLAM!
3-13
MOM SAYS NOT TO FLY YOUR KITE IN THE HOUSE..
SCHULZ

3-14
SCHULZ
IT'S ALMOST TIME FOR DINNER..
IF I MOVE, I'LL WAKE UP MY DOG..
PLEASE DON'T TALK..IT MAKES YOUR STOMACH GO UP AND DOWN, AND IT'S VERY DISTURBING

This is my report on dogs.

Dogs are good to have around because they are always alert.
Z

3-15
KLUNK!

Well, some of them are.
SCHULZ

3-16
SURPRISE! I DECORATED YOUR DINNER WITH A LITTLE FLAG!
IT LOOKS LIKE THE EIGHTH HOLE AT PEBBLE BEACH..
SCHULZ

POW!

HERE'S YOUR SOCK, CHARLIE BROWN..I COULDN'T GET THE BALL OUT..
SCHULZ
3-17

WELL, THAT'S IT, CHARLIE BROWN..WE LOST AGAIN

IN THE OLD DAYS, IF SOMEONE WAS DEFEATED, HE HELD UP A WHITE FLAG..

3-18
SCHULZ

Z
3-19

THE BALL WAS RIGHT OVER THE PLATE! WHY DIDN'T I SWING?!

Z
SCHULZ

PEANUTS
MY PITCHER'S MOUND LOOKS GREAT..

IT'S GOING TO BE A GOOD SEASON, CHARLIE BROWN!

OUR OL' BACKSTOP SEEMS TO BE IN GOOD SHAPE..

HOW ABOUT THE OUTFIELD?

ALL MOWED, CHARLIE BROWN..IT'S BEAUTIFUL!

AND WE'VE RAKED THE INFIELD SO IT LOOKS BETTER THAN EVER..
3-20

THEN ALL WE HAVE TO WORRY ABOUT IS THE SOUND SYSTEM..

THE SOUND SYSTEM?

THIS YEAR LET'S TRY TO GET THE BALL OVER THE PLATE, YOU BLOCKHEAD!

THE SOUND SYSTEM IS STILL WORKING..

I'M SORRY, MA'AM, IF MY TEST PAPER IS A LITTLE HARD TO READ...

I HAD TROUBLE WRITING IT BECAUSE THERE WAS SOMETHING ON MY DESK..
3-21

A HEAD!
Z
SCHULZ

HEY, CHUCK..I NEED YOUR HELP WITH A SCHOOL ASSIGNMENT

WE HAVE TO INTERVIEW A BUSINESSMAN..WHAT DOES YOUR DAD DO?

A BARBER? ASK HIM IF THAT'S A BUSINESS..
3-22

AN ART? WELL, I GUESS THAT'LL BE ALL RIGHT..
SCHULZ

EXCUSE ME.. IS THIS A BARBER SHOP?

SIR, MY NAME IS PATRICIA.. I'M A FRIEND OF YOUR SON, CHUCK, THE WEIRD KID...

ANYWAY, I'M HERE TO INTERVIEW YOU FOR A SCHOOL ASSIGNMENT
3-23

NO, YOU GO AHEAD AND CUT HAIR.. I'LL JUST STAND HERE AND WATCH...

SCHULZ

YES, SIR, I'M SUPPOSED TO INTERVIEW A BUSINESSMAN SO I HAVE THESE QUESTIONS...

HOW DID YOU GET STARTED AS A BARBER?

IS THERE ROOM FOR ADVANCEMENT? WHAT ABOUT HEALTH CARE? IS IT A GOOD CAREER FOR WOMEN?
3-24

Y'ALL COME BACK NOW, Y'HEAR?

YOU DID A NICE JOB ON THAT GUY..
SCHULZ

THIS IS MY REPORT ON THE BUSINESSMAN BARBER I INTERVIEWED..
3-25

YEARS AGO, HE SAID, HAIRCUTS WERE THIRTY-FIVE CENTS AND ICE CREAM CONES WERE A NICKEL..

BRINGS BACK A LOT OF MEMORIES FOR YOU, HUH, MA'AM?
SCHULZ

I THINK YOUR SHORTSTOP IS ASLEEP
IT'S THE DREAMING THAT GETS ME..
WOOF! WHIMPER.. WHINE... WHIMPER! WHIMPER!
SCHULZ
3-26

PEANUTS
by SCHULZ

THIS HAS BEEN A LONG UPHILL CLIMB..

BUT IT WAS WORTH IT, WASN'T IT?
3-27

OF COURSE, NOW WE HAVE THAT LITTLE PROBLEM OF GETTING DOWN..

SCHULZ

I'D HATE TO HAVE A JOB WHERE YOU HAD TO GET UP EARLY IN THE MORNING..
I'D HATE TO HAVE A JOB WHERE YOU STAYED IN THE SAME PLACE ALL DAY..
I'D HATE TO HAVE A JOB WHERE YOU HAD TO BE NICE TO EVERYBODY..
SCHULZ
3/28

SO WHAT I'M SAYING HERE IS WE CAN'T COMPARE APPLES AND WATERMELONS..

OR GRAPES, OR PEARS, OR BANANAS, OR PEACHES, OR STRAWBERRIES, OR..
3-29

MA'AM?

ORANGES, SIR..
FORGET IT, MARCIE
SCHULZ

3-30
HAS THE BUS COME YET?
IF THE BUS HAD COME, I'D BE ON IT, AND I'D BE HALF WAY TO SCHOOL BY NOW, AND I WOULDN'T BE HERE FOR YOU TO ASK ME!

CRABBY FLAKES FOR BREAKFAST AGAIN, HUH?
SCHULZ

AND IT SAYS HERE THAT NO ONE HAS BEEN KNOWN TO HAVE BEEN STRUCK BY A FALLING METEORITE..

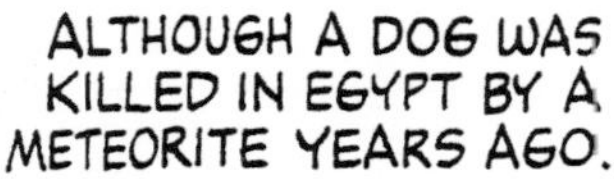
ALTHOUGH A DOG WAS KILLED IN EGYPT BY A METEORITE YEARS AGO..

WHAT DO THEY MEAN, "ALTHOUGH" A DOG?
SCHULZ
3-31

HERE'S THE FIERCE JUNGLE ANIMAL SNEAKING UP ON HIS PREY...

USING ALL HIS NATIVE CUNNING, HE CREEPS UP BEHIND HIS VICTIM...

IS THIS THE FRONT OR THE BACK?
4-1
SCHULZ

WHAT?
4-2

SORRY.. I CAN'T HEAR YOU WHEN THE WIND IS BLOWING!
SCHULZ

PEANUTS®

by SCHULZ

THESE ARE COMMAS.. IF A COMMA WORKS HARD, IT CAN BECOME AN APOSTROPHE, SEE?

The dog's bone.
The cat's whiskers.

IF A COMMA FINDS A PARTNER, IT CAN GO INTO PAIRS..THEY CAN BECOME QUOTATION MARKS..

AREN'T THE ONES ON THE LEFT UPSIDE DOWN?

TO BECOME A REAL QUOTATION MARK, THEY HAVE TO LEARN TO DO A BACKFLIP..

I'D BETTER GO.. I HAVE SOME WRITING TO DO FOR HOMEWORK
4-3

WATCH THOSE QUOTATION MARKS WHEN THEY DO A BACKFLIP..
SCHULZ

PSYCHIATRIC HELP 5¢
SOME DAYS I'M UP, AND THE NEXT DAYS I'M DOWN
THE DOCTOR IS IN

LIKE AN EMOTIONAL ROLLER COASTER, HUH?

DO YOU EVER FEEL LIKE YOU'RE ON A ROLLER COASTER, CHARLIE BROWN?
THE DOCTOR IS IN

HOW ABOUT BUMPER CARS?
SCHULZ
4-4

I WONDER HOW THE COMPOSER COULD WRITE SOMETHING SO BEAUTIFUL..

I WONDER HOW THE VIOLINIST CAN REMEMBER ALL THOSE NOTES..
4-5

I WONDER HOW THEY CHANGE THOSE LIGHT BULBS WAY UP THERE IN THE CEILING..
SCHULZ

HI, CHARLES..WE'VE JUST BEEN TO A LONG SYMPHONY CONCERT

4-6
WHAT'S WRONG WITH PATTY?
SHE WAS MAHLERED!
SCHULZ

CHARLIE BROWN? I HAPPENED TO BE WALKING BY, AND I SAW THIS KITE ALL TANGLED UP IN THIS BIG BUSH, AND I WAS JUST WONDERING HOW..
DON'T ASK!
4-7
SCHULZ

SOME THINGS RUN IN THE FAMILY..
RATS!
SCHULZ
4-8

4-9
I SEE YOUR OPPONENT HAS TO GIVE YOU TWO STROKES ON EVERY HOLE... DOES THAT BOTHER YOU?
JOE NO-PRIDE!
SCHULZ

PEANUTS®
by SCHULZ
I LOVE MEETINGS ON THE MOUND!

ONE FINGER WILL MEAN A FAST BALL, AND TWO FINGERS A CURVE BALL..
TELL YOUR CATCHER I THINK HE'S CUTE..

4-10

SCHULZ
Did you tell him I think he's cute?

NOW, AFTER WE TAKE FORT ZINDERNEUF, I HOPE A CERTAIN SOMEONE DOESN'T THINK WE'RE GOING TO HAVE A BIG PARTY..
4-11
SCHULZ

"WHAT'S THAT SUPPOSED TO MEAN?" THAT'S MY NEW PHILOSOPHY!

WHENEVER SOMEONE SAYS SOMETHING TO ME, I JUST SAY, "WHAT'S THAT SUPPOSED TO MEAN?"
4-12

I'M GLAD YOU TOLD ME..NOW I WON'T SAY ANYTHING TO YOU

WHAT'S THAT SUPPOSED TO MEAN?
SCHULZ

GUESS WHAT..

YOU'RE A DOG, AND YOU'LL ALWAYS BE A DOG!

HOW REASSURING!
SCHULZ
4-13

DID BEETHOVEN EVER DO ANY ENDORSEMENTS? YOU KNOW, LIKE TENNIS SHOES OR SOMETHING?

NO! BEETHOVEN NEVER ENDORSED ANY TENNIS SHOES!!
4-14

KLUNK

THAT'S TOO BAD.. BEETHOVEN TENNIS SHOES WOULD HAVE GONE OVER BIG
SCHULZ

4-15
I MUST ADMIT, SIR, THAT I NEVER WOULD HAVE THOUGHT TO PUT A WATERMELON IN MY LUNCH..
SCHULZ

"HOWEVER, THE BIG PROBLEM IS AN OVERTURNED RIG AT THE CORNER OF THIRD AND MISSION"
SCHULZ

4-16
NO, THE BIG PROBLEM IS I HAVEN'T DONE ANY HOMEWORK..

PEANUTS
by SCHULZ
OH, NO! LOOK WHO'S COMING..
THE DOCTOR IS IN

PSYCHIATRIC HELP 5¢
'PIGPEN,' YOU'RE A COMPLETE MESS!
THE DOCTOR IS IN

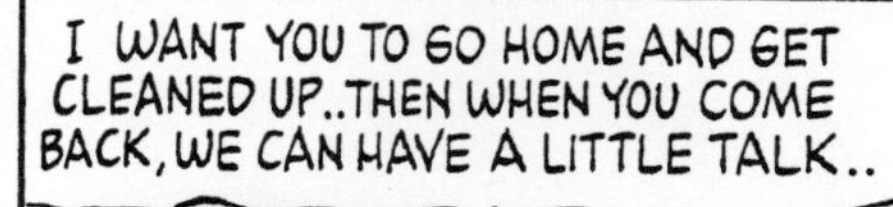
I WANT YOU TO GO HOME AND GET CLEANED UP..THEN WHEN YOU COME BACK, WE CAN HAVE A LITTLE TALK..

4-17

WOW! YOU LOOK GREAT! NOW WE CAN TALK ABOUT APPEARANCE, AND HOW IMPORTANT IT CAN BE...
THE DOCTOR

WE MAY NOT BELIEVE IT, BUT IT'S TRUE..
THE DOCTOR IS IN

WE MAY LIKE TO THINK APPEARANCE ISN'T..
THE DOCTOR IS IN

SIGH
THE DOCTOR IS IN
SCHULZ

4-18
OKAY, THERE'S FORT ZINDERNEUF! I NEED ONE VOLUNTEER TO GO AHEAD, AND DEMAND THEIR SURRENDER..

GOOD! IF THEY SURRENDER, THEY CAN HAVE A BALLOON
SCHULZ

YESTERDAY I STOOD HERE IN THE RAIN FOR TEN MINUTES WAITING FOR THE SCHOOL BUS..

AFTER I GOT TO SCHOOL, YOU KNOW WHAT I LEARNED? I LEARNED HOW WIDE THE MISSISSIPPI RIVER IS..

I STOOD IN THE RAIN FOR TEN MINUTES TO LEARN HOW WIDE THE MISSISSIPPI RIVER IS!

HOW WIDE IS THE MISSISSIPPI RIVER?
I FORGOT
SCHULZ
4/19

4-20
NEVER TRY TO KISS SOMEBODY THROUGH A CATCHER'S MASK!
SCHULZ

4-21

SHE CAUGHT IT!

REJOICE! "THOU SAWIST IT, AND DIDST REJOICE" I SAMUEL 19:5!

"AND THOU SHALT REJOICE IN EVERY GOOD THING" DEUTERONOMY 26:11

I HAVE A WEIRD TEAM..
SCHULZ

THROW IT, LUCY!

THROW THE BALL!
4-22

THROW IT! THROW IT! THROW IT!!

SORRY, MANAGER..IT TOOK ME A WHILE TO UNPLUG MY HAIR DRYER..
SCHULZ

SOMETIMES I LIE AWAKE AT NIGHT, AND I ASK, "WHY AM I HERE? WHAT'S THE PURPOSE OF IT ALL? DOES MY LIFE HAVE ANY MEANING?"

THEN A VOICE COMES TO ME THAT SAYS, "FORGET IT! I HATE QUESTIONS LIKE THAT!"
4-23
SCHULZ

YOU HAVE A STRANGE GALLERY..
PEANUTS
by SCHULZ

HERE'S THE WORLD FAMOUS GOLFER HITTING A BEAUTIFUL SHOT TO THE EIGHTEENTH GREEN..

HE MARKS HIS BALL WITH A CHOCOLATE-CHIP COOKIE..

THEN HE WALKS BACK TO GET HIS PUTTER..

4-24
NOW HE RETURNS TO THE GREEN TO SINK THE WINNING PUTT...

BUT THE BIRDS HAVE EATEN HIS BALL MARKER!
SCHULZ

4-25
CLICK!

I HAVE PHOTOS OF ALL MY SUPPER DISHES..

DO YOU WANT ONE FOR YOUR WALLET?
SCHULZ

I KNOW THE ANSWER! I KNOW THE ANSWER!

THE ANSWER IS, AS WE ALL KNOW FROM PREVIOUS GENERATIONS, AND PERSONAL EXPERIENCE, AND CLIMATE CONDITIONS, AND DIAGRAMS, AND..
4-26

SIX!
YES, THE ANSWER IS SIX..
SCHULZ

4-27
OKAY, SAY, "BIRDSEED"
SCHULZ

AS SISTER AND BROTHER, YOU KNOW WHAT OUR PROBLEM IS? WE DON'T TRY HARD ENOUGH TO GET ALONG..

I MEAN, I TRY, BUT YOU DON'T..
SO EVERYTHING IS REALLY MY FAULT?

NOW, YOU'RE TRYING!
SCHULZ
4-28

4-29
I WONDER WHAT IT WOULD BE LIKE TO BE A DOG AND NOT HAVE TO DO ANYTHING..
MAYBE THEY THINK OF BARKING AS BEING WORK..
WOOF!
WHEW THAT WAS EXHAUSTING!
SCHULZ

AS SISTER AND BROTHER, WE'RE ALMOST LIKE A TEAM..

I'M THE MANAGER, AND YOU'RE THE WORTHLESS PLAYER WHO IS GOOD FOR NOTHING EXCEPT SITTING ON THE BENCH!
4-30

IT'S GOING TO BE A LONG SEASON
SCHULZ

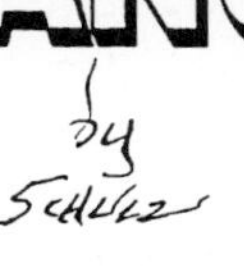
PEANUTS
by
SCHULZ

Z

YAWN

5-1
YAWN

SCHULZ

IF WE'RE A COUPLE OF FARM DOGS, OLAF, DON'T YOU THINK WE SHOULD BE DOING SOMETHING?

DON'T YOU THINK WE SHOULD BE USEFUL?
WE ARE USEFUL..

IF WE MOVE, THE BARN WILL FALL DOWN..
SCHULZ
5-2

5-3
CANOEING ALL THE WAY, HUH?

NO, THERE USED TO BE A CAMPGROUND DOWNSTREAM, BUT IT'S NOT THERE ANYMORE
SCHULZ

YOU KNOW, OLAF, WE SHOULD WRITE TO OUR BROTHER SNOOPY..

WE HAVEN'T SEEN HIM SINCE HE WAS IN THE HOSPITAL
5-4

I THINK I KNOW WHERE THERE'S SOME STATIONERY..

BUT WE'D ALSO NEED A PENCIL..
ARE THEY VERY HEAVY?
SCHULZ

ARE YOU PADDLING UPSTREAM OR DOWNSTREAM?

5-5

SCHULZ
SORRY.. I DIDN'T MEAN TO CONFUSE YOU..

I THINK SNOOPY WOULD ENJOY GETTING A LETTER FROM US
WE DON'T KNOW HOW TO WRITE, DO WE?

NO, REMEMBER WHAT I USED TO TELL YOU?
WHAT WAS THAT?

OBEDIENCE SCHOOL WAS A WASTE OF TIME!
5-6
SCHULZ

5-7
BE CAREFUL..

IF YOU PADDLE TO THE EDGE OF THE EARTH, YOU MIGHT FALL OFF..

SCHULZ

PEANUTS
by SCHULZ

?

HA! I MADE YOU LOOK!

HEE HEE HEE
5-8

YOU THINK I'M SO DUMB I'D FALL FOR MY OWN TRICK?

I'M NOT GONNA LOOK..

SCHULZ

HEY, MANAGER.. ASK YOUR CATCHER IF HE'S GOING TO TAKE ME TO THE SENIOR PROM!
5-9

SHE WANTS TO KNOW IF YOU'RE GOING TO TAKE HER TO THE SENIOR PROM..

HE SAYS NOT IF YOU WERE THE LAST PERSON ON EARTH!

I'LL CANCEL THE LIMO..
SCHULZ

MOVE AWAY.. I'M TRYING TO GET A TAN
I'M NOT BOTHERING YOU

YOU'RE USING UP ALL THE SUN!
5-10
SCHULZ

5-11
ALL RIGHT, TEAM, WE'RE ONLY ONE RUN BEHIND.. WE CAN WIN IF WE CONCENTRATE!
WE'RE CONCENTRATING!
WE'RE ALL CONCENTRATING..
Z
KLUNK!
SCHULZ

I'M DESPERATELY IN NEED OF HELP WITH MY HOMEWORK..

ALL RIGHT, BUT YOU'RE GOING TO HAVE TO PAY ATTENTION..

NOW, IN THIS FIRST PROBLEM, THE..

I HATE PAYING ATTENTION..
5/12
SCHULZ

HEY, PITCHER! YOU WANT SOME ADVICE?
5-13

WHAT KIND OF ADVICE COULD A PITCHER GET FROM AN OUTFIELDER?

YOU NEED A HAIRCUT!
SCHULZ

I HEAR YOU JUST LOST ANOTHER CASE..

IN THE OLD DAYS, WHEN AN ATTORNEY LOST A CASE, HE'D REND HIS GARMENTS..
5-14

NOWADAYS WE JUST KICK OUR HAT!
SCHULZ

PEANUTS
by SCHULZ

AAUGH!!
NOT AGAIN!

CAN'T YOU CATCH ANYTHING? HOW COULD YOU MISS IT?!

YOU'RE THE WORST PLAYER IN THE HISTORY OF THE GAME!

YOU'RE GOING TO DRIVE ME CRAZY!!

HOW CAN YOU BE SO BAD?!

5-15

ARE YOU TALKING TO ME?
SCHULZ

From the day I was born my life has been hard.

5-16
THIS IS RIDICULOUS! YOU HAVE AN EASY LIFE!

Starting now, my life has been very hard.
SCHULZ

5-17
DON'T YOU THINK YOU SHOULD YELL "FORE!"?
DOGS CAN'T TALK..
BONK
SCHULZ

One of my greatest thrills was being part of a dogsled team.
5-18

YOU WERE NEVER PART OF A DOGSLED TEAM..

Every winter the kid next door used to pull me on his sled.
SCHULZ

THIS IS MY REPORT ON HAMLET..

A HAMLET IS A SMALL VILLAGE WITH A POPULATION OF MAYBE A FEW HUNDRED, AND..
5-19

MA'AM?

FAR AND AWAY, SIR, ONE OF THE GREAT TRIES OF ALL TIME!
I CAN'T STAND IT..
SCHULZ

5-20
SCHULZ

5-21
I JUST CAN'T BELIEVE HOW STUPID YOUR STORIES ARE!

IN FACT, I CAN'T SEE ANYTHING GOOD AT ALL ABOUT YOUR WRITING!

I HAVE NEAT MARGINS..
SCHULZ

PEANUTS
by SCHULZ

SIT ON THE BALL, MARCIE, AND I'LL TAKE YOUR PICTURE
WHY DON'T I DO A SLAM-DUNK?

YOU COULDN'T SLAM-DUNK A DOUGHNUT! JUST SIT ON THE BALL!

MAYBE YOU'RE RIGHT, MARCIE.. HOW ABOUT A SLAM-KLUNK?
5-22
SCHULZ

5-23

SMALLEST DESERT I'VE EVER SEEN..
SCHULZ

5-24

WELL, DID YOU ENJOY THE BOOK ?

I DON'T KNOW..I SLEPT ALL THE WAY THROUGH IT..
SCHULZ

I NEED HELP WITH MY HOMEWORK
AGAIN?

YOU KNOW, I'M NOT ALWAYS GOING TO BE AROUND TO HELP YOU..

HOW OLD DO YOU THINK YOU'RE GOING TO BE BEFORE YOU WON'T NEED ME ANYMORE?

5-25
EIGHTY !
SCHULZ

DO YOU HAVE ANY REGRETS, CHARLIE BROWN?
LOTS OF THEM..
I REGRET THE BITES I SHOULD HAVE BITTEN..
5-26
SCHULZ

LOOK AT THIS, MARCIE! SHE GAVE ME A FAILING GRADE ON MY THEME!

I'M TOTALLY CRUSHED! I WAS SURE I WAS GOING TO GET A GOOD GRADE!

THIS IS A BLANK SHEET OF PAPER..

BUT THE POTENTIAL WAS THERE!!
5-27
SCHULZ

I HAVE SOMETHING TO SAY TO YOU THAT WILL MAKE YOUR HAIR STAND ON END..

I SAID IT WILL MAKE YOUR HAIR STAND ON END!

THAT'S BETTER..
5/28
SCHULZ

PEANUTS
by SCHULZ

LET ME EXPLAIN..
THE DOCTOR IS IN

PSYCHIATRIC HELP 5¢
IT'S A RELAXING TECHNIQUE
THE DOCTOR IS IN

I WANT YOU TO PICTURE YOURSELF STANDING IN A BEAUTIFUL MEADOW

IMAGINE THE SOFT RAYS OF THE SUN PENETRATING YOUR WHOLE BODY..

THEN TRY TO IMAGINE THE MOST WONDERFUL GENTLE BREEZE CARESSING YOUR UPTURNED FACE..

CAN YOU DO THAT, CHARLIE BROWN?
THE DOCTOR IS IN
5-29

YOU'RE STANDING OUT IN THIS BEAUTIFUL MEADOW..WHAT ARE YOU THINKING?

IT'S ONLY THE FIRST INNING, AND THE OTHER TEAM HAS ALREADY SCORED FORTY RUNS!
THE DOCTOR
SCHULZ

5-30
SOME PRETTY BIG ONES IN THERE, HUH?
SCHULZ

ROOM SERVICE!
SCHULZ
5-31
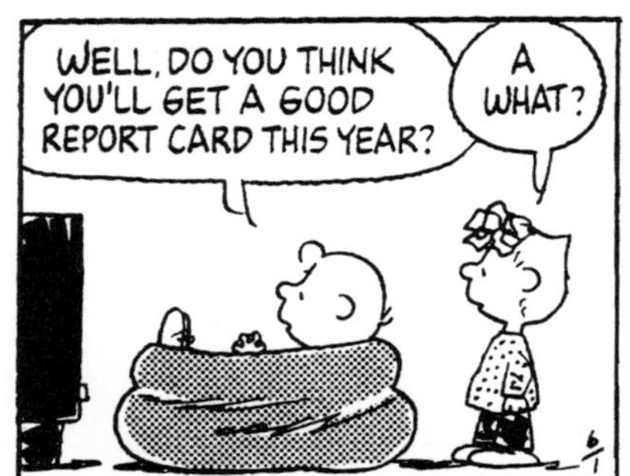
WELL, DO YOU THINK YOU'LL GET A GOOD REPORT CARD THIS YEAR?
A WHAT?
6/1

A REPORT CARD.. YOU KNOW, GRADES.. "A, B, C, D."..

SOME SCHOOLS JUST GIVE "SATISFACTORY" OR "UNSATISFACTORY"
HOW ABOUT, "THANKS FOR BEING HERE"?
SCHULZ

SOMETIMES I LIE AWAKE AT NIGHT, AND I ASK, "WHO, WHY, WHAT AND WHERE?"

THEN A VOICE COMES BACK TO ME THAT SAYS, "WAIT A MINUTE..I THINK YOU'VE LOST ME"
6-2
SCHULZ

THIS IS YOUR REPORT CARD? YOU GOT ALL "A'S"! WOW! HOW DID YOU DO IT?

I'M A GOOD STUDENT... I SHOW UP ON TIME, AND I DO WHAT I'M TOLD...

6-3
AND I COLOR BETWEEN THE LINES!
SCHULZ

HERE, I THOUGHT YOU MIGHT LIKE TO SEE THE MENU FOR NEXT WEEK

"DOG FOOD, DOG FOOD, DOG FOOD, DOG FOOD, DOG FOOD, DOG FOOD AND DOG FOOD"

6-4
NO SHERBET TO CLEANSE THE PALATE?
SCHULZ

PEANUTS
by SCHULZ

ANOTHER ROOT BEER, PLEASE..

THIS IS MY REPORT ON "D-DAY," JUNE 6, 1944..

FIFTY YEARS AGO THE ALLIES WERE POISED TO BEGIN THE INVASION OF NORMANDY..

NO ONE, HOWEVER, KNEW WHEN THAT DAY WOULD BE..

NO ONE BUT AN UNKNOWN SOLDIER SITTING IN A TINY PUB DRINKING ROOT BEER WHO CAME TO A STARTLING CONCLUSION..

"FELDMARSCHALL" ROMMEL IS IN CHARGE OF DEFENDING THE BEACHES OF NORMANDY..

BUT HIS WIFE'S BIRTHDAY IS JUNE 6 !! HE'S SURE TO GO HOME FOR HER BIRTHDAY! HE WON'T BE IN NORMANDY!!

THE UNKNOWN UNSUNG HERO RUSHED TO A PHONE TO CALL GENERAL EISENHOWER

"D-DAY HAS TO BE JUNE 6!

SPEAKING IN CODE, THE SIMPLE SOLDIER MADE A PHONE CALL THAT CHANGED THE COURSE OF HISTORY..
6-5

TELEPHONE
WOOF!
SCHULZ

IT'S D-DAY! HERE'S THE WORLD FAMOUS G.I. CHARGING THROUGH THE SURF AT OMAHA BEACH!
6/6

HEY, CHARLES, YOUR DOG IS OVER HERE RUNNING BACK AND FORTH THROUGH OUR WADING POOL..
SCHULZ

D+2! THE WORLD FAMOUS G.I. DIGS A FOXHOLE..
6/7

HEY, CHARLIE BROWN, YOUR DOG IS DIGGING IN OUR BACKYARD!
SCHULZ

D+3..THE WORLD FAMOUS G.I. COMES ACROSS AN ABANDONED JEEP
6/8

HEY, CHUCK, WHY IS YOUR DOG SITTING OUT HERE IN A GROCERY CART?
SCHULZ

D+4! THE BRAVE INFANTRYMAN HURLS A GRENADE AT THE PILLBOX! THEN ANOTHER..AND ANOTHER!
6/9

WHY DO I HAVE THE FEELING SOMEONE IS THROWING ROCKS AT OUR FRONT DOOR?
SCHULZ

Dear Mom, Just a note to tell you I am well. They say we will be home by Christmas. I hope so.
6-10 SCHULZ

IT SAYS HERE THAT WHEN BEETHOVEN WROTE THIS SYMPHONY, HE DEDICATED IT TO NAPOLEON...

BUT WHEN NAPOLEON PROCLAIMED HIMSELF EMPEROR, BEETHOVEN TORE UP THE DEDICATION
6-11

GOOD FOR HIM!

WHO WAS NAPOLEON?
SCHULZ

PEANUTS®
by SCHULZ

THIS IS A GOOD GAME, RERUN..

HERE, YOU TAKE THIS PACK OF CARDS..

6-12
AND I'LL PUT THIS BASKET OVER HERE...

NOW, SEE HOW MANY CARDS YOU CAN THROW INTO THE BASKET..

SCHULZ

I GUESS MAYBE THEY'RE RIGHT.. GOLF IS A GAME OF INCHES..
6-13
SCHULZ

DID YOU KNOW THERE ARE 600,000 DOCTORS IN THIS COUNTRY ?

AS A WORLD FAMOUS SURGEON, DO YOU THINK THAT'S TOO MANY DOCTORS?

ONLY IF THEY'RE ALL ON CALL TONIGHT..
SCHULZ
6-14

WHEN YOU WALK THROUGH A STORM, IS IT TRUE YOU SHOULDN'T BE AFRAID?
NOT IF YOU HAVE HOPE..
WHY DO THEY SAY, "YOU'LL NEVER WALK ALONE"?
IF YOU'RE LUCKY, YOUR DOG WILL BE WITH YOU..
6-15
SCHULZ

ARE YOU AND YOUR DOG GOING TO CAMP THIS SUMMER, CHARLIE BROWN?
6-16

I DON'T KNOW.. I'M NEVER QUITE SURE HOW HE FEELS ABOUT IT...

I'D RATHER GO TO AFRICA, AND GET EATEN BY AN ELEPHANT..
SCHULZ

MAYBE WE SHOULD GO TO SUMMER CAMP AFTER ALL.. I'VE BEEN LOOKING AT THIS BROCHURE...

THEY HAVE TEN CABINS, AND EACH CABIN HAS SIX BUNK BEDS..
6-17

SURE, AND THE DOG SLEEPS ON THE FLOOR..
SCHULZ

OKAY, SNOOPY, WE'RE ALL SET TO GO!

WOW! ARE YOU SURE YOU'RE BRINGING ENOUGH STUFF?

I'M GLAD YOU REMINDED ME..I FORGOT MY BOWLING BALL!
SCHULZ
6-18

PEANUTS
by
SCHULZ

ALL RIGHT, LET'S WAKE UP OUT THERE!

HEY, MANAGER! YOU KNOW WHAT WE SHOULD HAVE?

WE SHOULD HAVE SCORECARDS

SCORECARDS?
"GET YOUR LUCKY NUMBER SCORECARD HERE!"

"YOU CAN'T TELL A PLAYER WITHOUT A SCORECARD!"
6-19

HAVING SEEN YOU PLAY, ARE YOU SURE YOU WANT EVERYONE TO KNOW WHO YOU ARE?

"DON'T GET YOUR SCORECARDS HERE!"
SCHULZ

THE BUS IS STOPPING..THIS MUST BE THE CAMP...

ARE YOU SURE YOU HAVE EVERYTHING? I THOUGHT YOU WERE GOING TO BRING YOUR BOWLING BALL..

6-20
SCHULZ

HI, GUYS! WELCOME TO CAMP!
6-21

YOU CAME IN ON THE BUS TOGETHER, HUH?

WHY IS THE LITTLE KID WEARING A DOG SUIT?
SCHULZ

HEY, LOOK, EVERYBODY! THIS KID BROUGHT A BOWLING BALL TO CAMP!

WHAT ARE YOU GONNA DO WITH THE BOWLING BALL, KID?
6-22

AAUGH
KLUNK!
SCHULZ

SNOOPY! SWIMMING LESSONS DOWN IN THE LAKE RIGHT AWAY!

ARE'T YOU GOING TO UNPACK?
6-23
SCHULZ

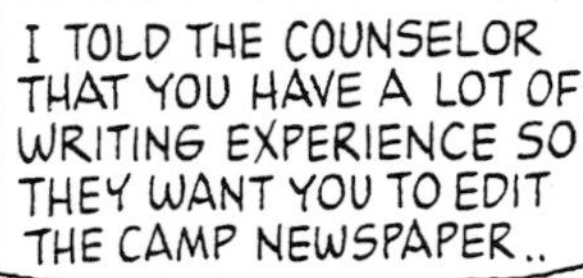
I TOLD THE COUNSELOR THAT YOU HAVE A LOT OF WRITING EXPERIENCE SO THEY WANT YOU TO EDIT THE CAMP NEWSPAPER..

Well, gang, this has been a great week at camp, right?

Personally, I would rather have gone to Africa and been eaten by an elephant.
6-24

SCHULZ

THE BEST PART OF GOING TO CAMP IS THE BUS RIDE HOME..

I HAVE TO ASK YOU AGAIN.. YOU DIDN'T FORGET YOUR BOWLING BALL, DID YOU?

6-25
SCHULZ

PEANUTS
by
SCHULZ

6-26

SCHULZ

SCHULZ 6-27
MY GRAMPA SAYS WHEN HE WAS LITTLE, KIDS USED TO ROLL HOOPS, SHOOT MARBLES AND SPIN TOPS..
AT THE MALL?

WE LOST AGAIN!
6-28

I CAN'T STAND IT!

FORTUNATELY, THAT'S VERY FUNNY!
SCHULZ

6-29

OKAY, SO YOU LOOK FIERCE GUARDING OUR BACK YARD..

WHAT IF SOMEONE COMES INTO OUR FRONT YARD?

SEND THEM AROUND HERE IN BACK..
SCHULZ

OKAY, I TIED MY OWN SHOES...NOW WHAT?

NOW, YOU CAN WALK, OR RUN, OR JUMP, OR DO ANYTHING YOU WANT..
6-30

YOU MEAN I DON'T HAVE TO GET PERMISSION?
SCHULZ

HI! MY NAME IS RERUN..I'VE NEVER BEEN TO THIS PLAYGROUND BEFORE..
7-1

I CAN TIE MY OWN SHOES!
MOM!
SCHULZ

WOODSTOCK ALWAYS TELLS SUCH SAD STORIES..
7-2

SNIF

DOGS DON'T HAVE HANDKERCHIEFS
SCHULZ

PEANUTS
by Schulz
HELLO?

LONG DISTANCE? HOW LONG?

HI, CHUCK! WE'RE HERE AT CAMP..DO YOU MISS ME?
US!

SURE WISH YOU WERE HERE WITH ME..
US!
7-3

SO WHAT DO YOU THINK, CHUCK? ARE YOU ANXIOUS TO SEE ME AGAIN?
US!

ANYWAY, CHUCK, I'VE ENJOYED TALKING WITH YOU..
WE'VE!

"WE'VE"?

WHO WAS ON THE PHONE?
IT SHOULD HAVE BEEN A WRONG NUMBER..
SCHULZ

TODAY IS A HOLIDAY SO I GUESS THE COURTHOUSE IS CLOSED..
7-4

I KNOW.. I HAVE TO GO ALL DAY WITHOUT SUING SOMEBODY

ATTORNEYS LOOK PATHETIC WHEN THE COURTHOUSE IS CLOSED..
TWENTY-FOUR HOURS DOWN THE DRAIN!
SCHULZ

THE COUNSELOR WANTS YOU TO LEAD IN OUR BREAKFAST PRAYER, SIR

DEAR LORD, THANK YOU FOR THESE PANCAKES.. AMEN!

NO ONE CAN ACCUSE YOU OF VAIN REPETITIONS, CAN THEY, SIR?
7/5

THE PANCAKES WERE GETTING COLD..
SCHULZ

HI, CHUCK! IT'S MARCIE AND I CALLING FROM CAMP AGAIN!

LOTS OF CUTE GUYS HERE, CHUCK, AND THEY ALL THINK MARCIE AND I ARE REALLY SOMETHING!

WHAT'S HE SAYING?
HE'S NOT SAYING ANYTHING..
7/6

GET JEALOUS, CHUCK!
SCHULZ

I'M WRITING A POST CARD TO CHARLES..

TELL HIM WE DON'T MISS HIM, AND WE DON'T CARE IF WE NEVER SEE HIM AGAIN!

7-7
AND TO SEND US SOME COOKIES..
SCHULZ

HERE, YOU GOT A POST CARD FROM SOME OF YOUR WEIRD GIRLFRIENDS AT SOME WEIRD CAMP..

YOU'VE ALREADY READ IT?!
7-8

I'VE ALREADY ANSWERED IT!
SCHULZ

YOU WROTE A POST CARD TO PATTY AND MARCIE, AND SIGNED MY NAME?!.
WHY NOT?

7-9
WELL, WHAT DID YOU SAY ON IT?
"DEAR DUMB GIRLS"
SCHULZ

PEANUTS®
by SCHULZ

CLOMP!

!
7-10

STUPID DOG!
SCHULZ

LOOK, I BOUGHT YOU A NEW BRAND OF DOG FOOD..
7-11

IT'S CALLED, "THE SAME OLD THING"

SO EVERY NIGHT AT SUPPERTIME YOU KNOW YOU'LL BE EATING "THE SAME OLD THING"

CALL THE AD AGENCY BEFORE IT'S TOO LATE..
SCHULZ

BY THE TIME I GET THERE, ALL THE HOT WATER WILL BE GONE..
7-12
SCHULZ

"The Untold Story of

DON'T TELL IT!

RATS!
7-13
SCHULZ

POW!

DO YOU THINK BASEBALLS ARE LIVELIER THAN THEY USED TO BE, CHARLIE BROWN?

NO, BUT I AM!
7-14
SCHULZ

SOMETIMES I LIE AWAKE AT NIGHT, AND I ASK, "WHERE HAVE I GONE WRONG?"
7-15

THEN A VOICE SAYS TO ME, "THIS IS GOING TO TAKE MORE THAN ONE NIGHT"
SCHULZ

TIME OUT!
?

AS TEAM MANAGER, MAY I ASK YOU SOMETHING?
Z
7-16

COULD YOU PLEASE STOP THINKING SLEEPING, AND THINK BASEBALL?
Z

SCHULZ

PEANUTS
SCHULZ

IT'S NOT THAT I DON'T APPRECIATE THE HOME I ALREADY HAVE..
BUT..

WHEN YOU'RE A DOG, SOMETIMES IT'S A GOOD IDEA TO SIT IN THE RAIN RIGHT NEXT TO THE CURB..

IT'S ALSO A GOOD IDEA TO LOOK REAL PATHETIC..

MAYBE A RICH LADY IN A BIG LIMOUSINE WILL STOP AND PICK YOU UP..

THEN SHE'LL TAKE YOU HOME TO HER FANCY APARTMENT, WRAP YOU IN A WARM FUZZY TOWEL AND GIVE YOU A PIZZA!

IS THIS HER I SEE COMING? IS SHE THE ONE I'VE BEEN WAITING FOR?

RATS!
SCHULZ
7-17

HELLO?

HI, CHUCK! JUST THOUGHT I'D LET YOU KNOW I'M BACK FROM CAMP..

I HAD A NICE TIME.. DID YOU MISS ME, CHUCK?
7-18

WHO IS THIS?

I'VE NEVER HEARD OF YOU EITHER, CHUCK!
SCHULZ

7-19
VERY STRANGE.. SOMEBODY SPILLED BIRDS ALL OVER THE YARD..
SCHULZ

HOW'S THIS, MANAGER?

SEE HOW I'M LOOKING UP?

PRETTY GOOD, HUH?
7-20

IF A FLY BALL COMES MY WAY, I'M READY!
SCHULZ

ALL MY LIFE I'VE BEEN WAITING FOR THAT "PIE IN THE SKY"

7-21
WHEN IT CAME, IT HAD COCONUT ON IT..
SCHULZ

PLUNK!
7-22

SCHULZ

SO HERE I AM RIDING ON THE BACK OF MY MOM'S BICYCLE ON THE WAY TO THE DRY CLEANERS..

MOM ALWAYS LIKES TO RETURN THE USED COAT HANGERS

7-23
SHE HATES IT WHEN I DO THIS..
SCHULZ

PEANUTS
by SCHULZ
7-24
JOE PILOT!
SCHULZ

7-25
LOOK, NEW SUPPER DISHES!

BLUE! GREEN! YELLOW! SILVER! PINK! A DIFFERENT COLOR FOR EVERY NIGHT!

SUDDENLY I'M IN THE FAST LANE..

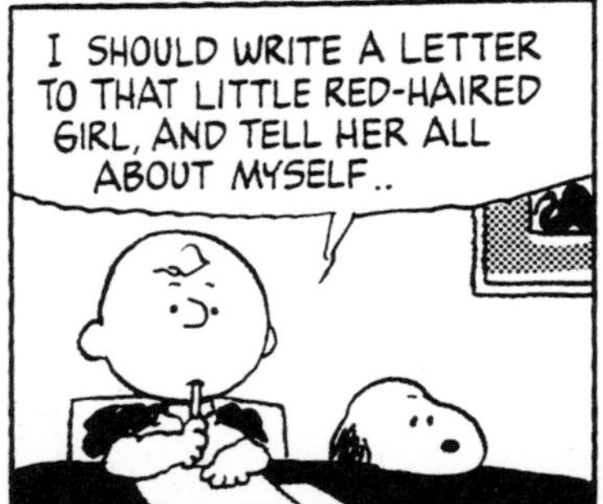
I SHOULD WRITE A LETTER TO THAT LITTLE RED-HAIRED GIRL, AND TELL HER ALL ABOUT MYSELF..

I COULD TELL HER HOW DEPENDABLE AND RELIABLE I AM..

LAST NIGHT MY SUPPER WAS ELEVEN SECONDS LATE!
7-26

SEE, RERUN? IT'S A JUMP ROPE..

YOU TWIRL THE ROPE, AND YOU JUMP UP AND DOWN LIKE THIS...

THEN YOU COUNT HOW MANY TIMES YOU JUMP..

7-27
WHY?

THIS IS HOW WE SHOOT BASKETS, RERUN

SEE, WE BOUNCE THE BALL A COUPLE OF TIMES TO GET OUR RHYTHM..

THEN WE FLIP IT THROUGH THE BASKET!

7-28
WHY?

OKAY, RERUN, I'M GOING TO READ YOU THIS STORY, AND IF YOU SAY, "WHY?" I'M GONNA POUND YOU!
7/29

HOW COME?

7-30
IF I EVER GOT A DOG, I'M NOT SURE WHAT KIND I'D GET..
THEY SAY THAT BORDER COLLIES ARE GOOD DOGS..
IF YOU DON'T MIND SOMEONE STARING AT YOU ALL THE TIME..

PEANUTS.
by
SCHULZ

HEY, MANAGER, IT'S PRETTY HOT TODAY, ISN'T IT?
?

BUT NOT FOR ME..I'VE GOT THIS PROBLEM LICKED..

I SOAKED THIS TOWEL IN COLD WATER, AND I'M AS COOL AS A CUCUMBER UNDER HERE!

YOU SHOULD HAVE ALL YOUR PLAYERS DO THIS..

7-31

CAFE

BONK!

I CAN'T BELIEVE IT..WHILE I WAS GONE, SOMEBODY PUT A MAILBOX IN RIGHT FIELD!
SCHULZ

IF I WRITE A LOVE NOTE TO THAT LITTLE RED-HAIRED GIRL, WILL YOU DELIVER IT FOR ME?
8-1

IF I GET CAPTURED, DO I HAVE TO SWALLOW IT?

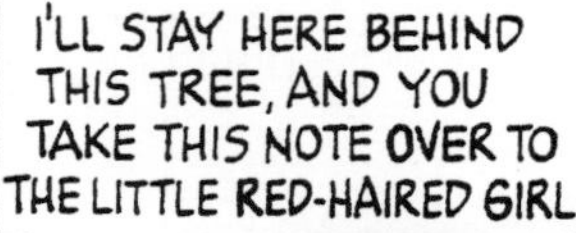
I'LL STAY HERE BEHIND THIS TREE, AND YOU TAKE THIS NOTE OVER TO THE LITTLE RED-HAIRED GIRL

8-2

GOOD MORNING, I HAVE A LOVE NOTE FOR YOU FROM MY WEIRD BROTHER..HE THINKS YOU'RE KIND OF CUTE

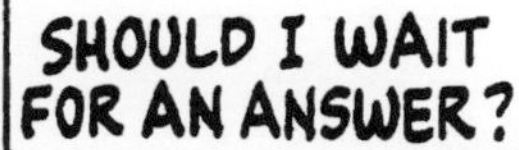
SHOULD I WAIT FOR AN ANSWER?

SHE'S READING YOUR LOVE NOTE!
8-3

DID YOU HEAR ME? ARE YOU STILL BEHIND THE TREE? WAVE YOUR HAND!

HE'S STILL THERE..REALLY? OH, SURE, I UNDERSTAND..

SHE SAID SHE COULDN'T READ YOUR SMUDGY WRITING...

AND WHEN I TOLD HER YOU'RE IN THE SAME CLASS AT SCHOOL, SHE SAID SHE DIDN'T REMEMBER YOU..
I CAN'T STAND IT!

8-4
MAYBE YOU SHOULD GIVE UP THIS INSANE LOVE AFFAIR.. JUST LET THINGS HAPPEN..THAT'S WHAT I'VE DONE WITH MY SWEET BABBOO...
I'M NOT YOUR SWEET BABBOO!
SCHULZ

BEETHOVEN HAD AN UNFORTUNATE LOVE AFFAIR TOO, CHARLIE BROWN..
8-5

BUT IT DIDN'T DISCOURAGE HIM.. HE KEPT RIGHT ON WORKING..

STRIKE THIS NEXT GUY OUT, AND YOU WON'T FEEL SO DEPRESSED..

POW!

BEETHOVEN PROBABLY HAD A BETTER CURVE BALL..
SCHULZ

I HAVE A NEW SYSTEM.. FIRST, I TEE UP THE BALL...
8-6

THEN I WALK AWAY FROM IT

I PAUSE FOR A MOMENT..

THEN I TURN AROUND AND LOOK

IF THE BALL HASN'T LEFT, I GO BACK AND HIT IT!
SCHULZ

PEANUTS
by SCHULZ

EVERYBODY OVER HERE!
ON THE DOUBLE!

ALL RIGHT, TROOPS.. BEFORE WE BEGIN OUR HIKE, I WANT ALL OF YOU TO SIGN THIS PAPER..

IF ANYONE GETS HURT, I AM NOT RESPONSIBLE..
8-7

WHAT'S THIS?

" IF WE GET TOTALLY LOST, AND FREEZE TO DEATH, AND NO ONE EVER SEES US AGAIN AND WE MISS ALL OUR TV PROGRAMS, OUR LEADER IS RESPONSIBLE "

ALL RIGHT, I'LL SIGN THAT, BUT YOU HAVE TO SIGN THIS OTHER ONE..

OKAY, YOU SIGN THIS ONE AND I'LL SIGN THAT ONE..

ALL RIGHT, THEN YOU SIGN THAT ONE AND I'LL SIGN THIS ONE..

WELL, HOW DID THE HIKE GO?
WE NEVER GOT OUT OF THE BACK YARD!
SCHULZ

Dear Editor,
I am sending you my latest novel.
8-8

HERE, THIS JUST CAME FOR YOU..

Don't!
SCHULZ

8-9
MAYBE YOU SHOULD WRITE A BIBLICAL NOVEL..

YOU KNOW, A STORY ABOUT SOMEONE LIKE JOHN THE BAPTIST..

John the Beagle
SCHULZ

HI, MARCIE.. ARE YOU AWAKE?
8-10

I'M AWAKE BECAUSE YOU'RE CALLING ME AT ONE IN THE MORNING!

CAN'T SLEEP EITHER, HUH?
SCHULZ

HI, CHUCK..SORRY TO WAKE YOU UP, BUT I COULDN'T SLEEP..
8-11

I'VE HAD A LOT ON MY MIND LATELY...

I LIKE TO TALK TO YOU BECAUSE YOU'RE ALWAYS A GOOD LISTENER..

Z
SCHULZ
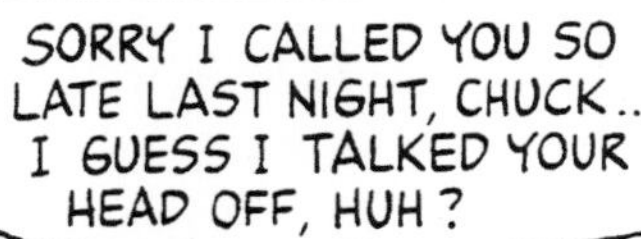
SORRY I CALLED YOU SO LATE LAST NIGHT, CHUCK.. I GUESS I TALKED YOUR HEAD OFF, HUH?

8-12

SOMETIMES I CAN'T SLEEP, AND I NEED TO TALK.. I LOVE TO TALK..

SOMETIMES I JUST NEED SOMEONE TO TALK TO..
SCHULZ

SCHULZ

8-13

"GIRL..A FEMALE CHILD
OR YOUNG PERSON"

PEANUTS

by SCHULZ

"DOG..A DOMESTICATED
CARNIVORE"

"FETCH..TO GO FOR,
AND BRING BACK"

THANK YOU..THAT WAS
GOOD FETCHING
"FETCHING..
CHARMING
AND
CAPTIVATING"
SCHULZ

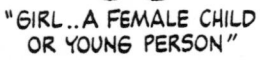

HI, MARCIE..DO YOU HAVE ANYTHING GOOD TO READ?

IT'S THREE O'CLOCK IN THE MORNING! WHY ARE YOU CALLING ME AT THREE O'CLOCK IN THE MORNING?!

I CAN'T SLEEP SO I THOUGHT I'D READ A BIT..

WAIT A MINUTE.. I THINK THERE'S SOMEONE AT THE DOOR...
8-15

HERE! READ THESE!!
SCHULZ

8-16
SCHULZ

8-17
DOES HAVING A DOG MAKE YOUR LIFE BETTER?
ABSOLUTELY! DOGS PROTECT YOU, GIVE YOU COMFORT, LOVE, JOY AND COMPANIONSHIP.. THAT'S THEIR JOB..
TALK ABOUT STRESS!
SCHULZ

8-18

I DIDN'T SLEEP WELL LAST NIGHT.. I COULDN'T GET COMFORTABLE..
SCHULZ

..AND SOME PENCILS, SOME PAPER, A PEN AND A LOOSE-LEAF BINDER..

CAN YOU THINK OF ANYTHING ELSE I MIGHT NEED FOR SCHOOL?
8-19

ASK HIM IF HE SELLS BRAINS..
IGNORE HER, SIR.. SHE'S EXCESSIVELY WEIRD!
SCHULZ

OKAY, LITTLE BROTHER, RUN OUT TO THE KITCHEN, AND GET ME A GLASS OF WATER..

WHY SHOULD I?
TO KEEP FROM GETTING POUNDED ON THE HEAD!
8-20

BROTHER HARASSMENT!!
SCHULZ

PEANUTS
by
SCHULZ

8-21

REMOTE CONTROLLED WOODSTOCK..
SCHULZ

8-22
YOU SHOULD WRITE ABOUT SOMETHING PLEASANT

WRITE SOMETHING THAT YOU KNOW WILL MAKE EVERYONE HAPPY..

The cat left the room.
SCHULZ

8-23

DON'T BE DISCOURAGED.. I'M NEW AT THIS..
SCHULZ

SEE? YOU HAVE FIVE TOES ON THIS FOOT AND FIVE TOES ON THAT FOOT..

8-24
IT'S A TIE!

IF THERE'S A PLAY-OFF, I'M IN TROUBLE..
SCHULZ

8-25
SOME PEOPLE THINK CATS ARE SMARTER THAN DOGS..
SOME PEOPLE THINK BIRDS AND DOGS ARE SMARTER THAN CATS..
WHY DO THEY THINK THAT?
CATS DON'T WEAR VISORS
SCHULZ

HI, CHUCK.. I COULDN'T SLEEP AGAIN SO I THOUGHT I'D CALL YOU..

I GUESS I LIE AWAKE AND WORRY ABOUT TOO MANY THINGS, HUH?

MAYBE ALL I NEED IS A KIND WORD... DO YOU HAVE A KIND WORD FOR ME, CHUCK?

WOOF!
8/26
SCHULZ

8-27

ALWAYS RUNS AROUND HIS BACKHAND..
SCHULZ

PEANUTS
by SCHULZ

BEWARE OF SNAKES
BRING OUT THE MONGOOSE!
8-28
SCHULZ

HEY, MARCIE..YOU WANNA HEAR THE EXCUSE I'VE COME UP WITH FOR MISSING SCHOOL?

YOU DON'T NEED AN EXCUSE, SIR.. WE'RE ON SUMMER VACATION..
8-29

WE ARE?

NO WONDER I'VE BEEN HOME A LOT LATELY..
SCHULZ

8-30

WE DON'T HAVE TO DO THIS, YOU KNOW..

IF YOU WERE A BORDER COLLIE, YOU'D BE OUT HERDING SHEEP..

8-31
I CAN DO THAT..

THIS WAY
SCHULZ

WELL, I'LL SAY THIS FOR YOU..YOU'RE VERY PATIENT..

LOOK, THERE'S SOME SHEEP!

IF YOU'RE A BORDER COLLIE, GO HERD THEM..

THEY TOLD ME TO GET LOST..

YOU'RE THE WORLD FAMOUS SURGEON, IS THAT RIGHT ?

BUT BEFORE PATIENTS CAN COME TO YOU, THEY HAVE TO GET PERMISSION FROM THEIR "PRIMARY CARE PHYSICIAN"

AND THEIR MOM

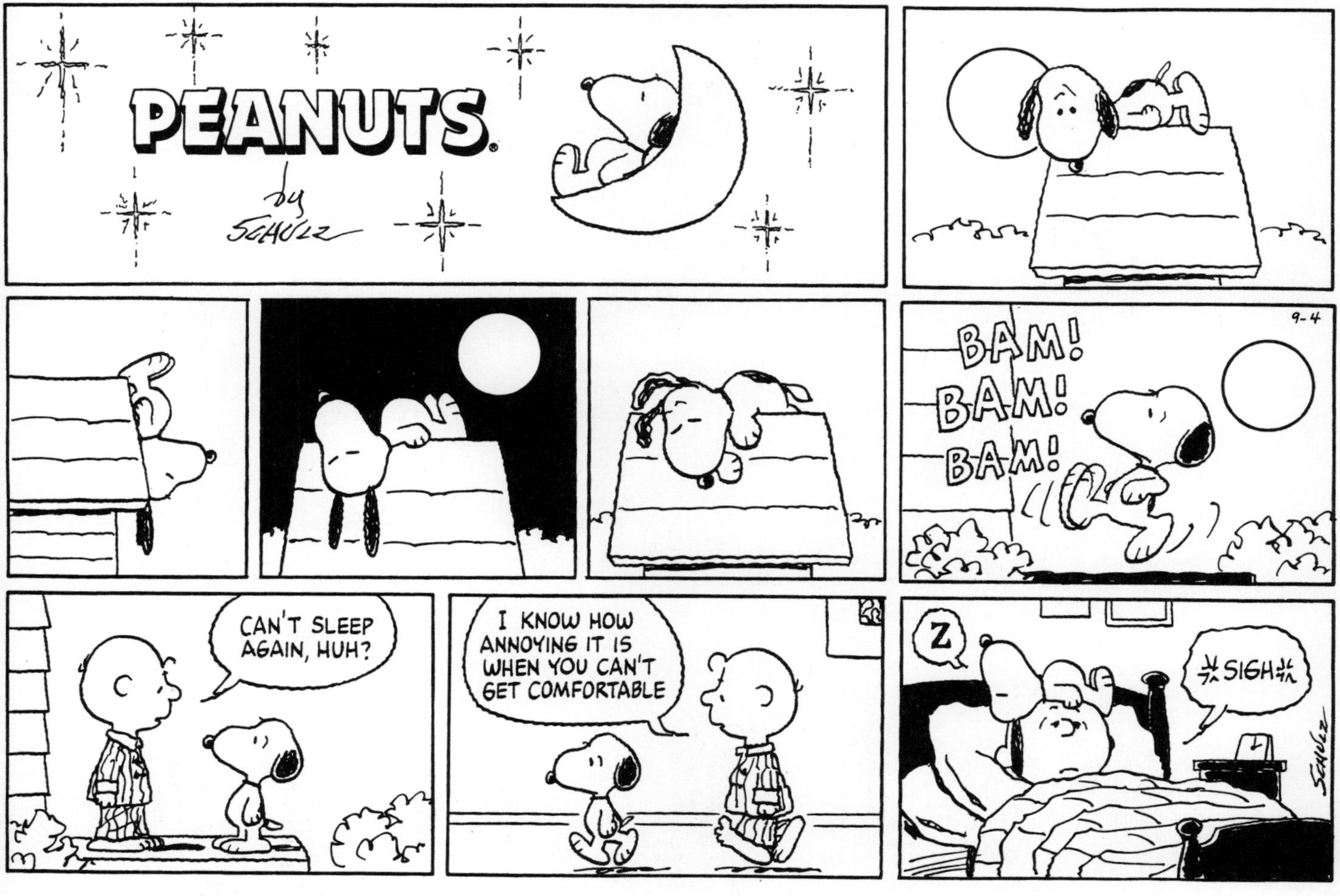

PEANUTS®

by SCHULZ

9-4

BAM!
BAM!
BAM!

CAN'T SLEEP AGAIN, HUH?

SORRY I MISSED THAT FLY BALL, MANAGER..
9-5

SO WHAT'S YOUR EXCUSE THIS TIME?

A VAPOR TRAIL GOT IN MY EYES..
SCHULZ

SCHOOL STARTS TOMORROW!

SHARPEN THOSE PENCILS! READ THOSE BOOKS! MAKE THOSE LUNCHES!

DREAD THOSE MORNINGS!
SCHULZ
9-6

GUESS WHAT, MARCIE.. I'M GOING FOR THE "MOST IMPROVED STUDENT" AWARD..

SCHOOL JUST STARTED TODAY, SIR..
9-7

AND I'M ALREADY BETTER THIS AFTERNOON THAN I WAS THIS MORNING..
SCHULZ

HERE, I BROUGHT YOUR LUNCH BAG FOR YOU
THANK YOU.. WHAT'S IN IT?
9-8

IN IT?
SCHULZ

LOOK, I BOUGHT YOU A SET OF LEGAL PADS..

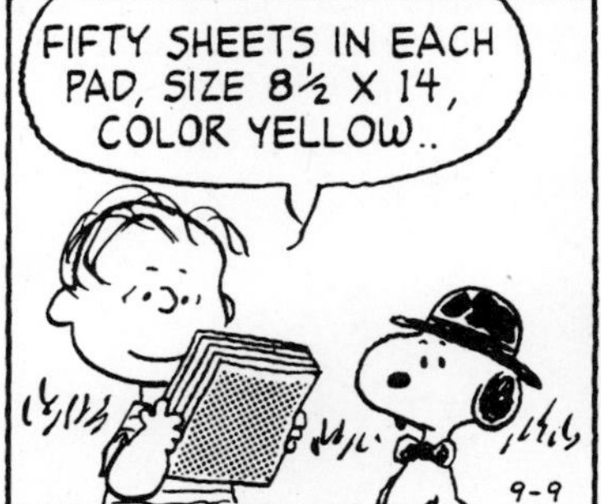
FIFTY SHEETS IN EACH PAD, SIZE 8½ X 14, COLOR YELLOW..
9-9

THE SORT OF MOMENT ALL ATTORNEYS DREAM ABOUT!
SCHULZ

THIS IS THE BIBLE VERSE I HAVE TO MEMORIZE FOR SUNDAY SCHOOL..

"REMEMBER LOT'S WIFE"
THAT'S VERY GOOD..
9-10

THANK YOU.. HOW ABOUT HELPING ME MAKE SOME CUE CARDS?
SCHULZ

PEANUTS
by SCHULZ
Sorry
Sorry
Sorry
Sorry
Sorry
Sorry
Sorry
Sorry
Sorry
Sorry
Sorry
Sorry
Dear Contributor,
We're sorry.
Your submission does not suit our present needs.
the Editors

I HAVE SOME ADVICE FOR YOU..

ALL THE BEST SELLERS THESE DAYS ARE ABOUT ATTORNEYS..

SO THAT'S WHO YOU SHOULD WRITE ABOUT..

It was a dark and stormy night.
9-11

Suddenly, an attorney appeared on the horizon.
SCHULZ

9-12
THE WORLD IS FILLED WITH MONDAYS..
SCHULZ

WHAT DID SHE SAY, MARCIE?

SHE WAS QUOTING FROM I KINGS, CHAPTER 18, VERSE 26..
9-13

"BUT THERE WAS NOT A SOUND; NO ONE ANSWERED, AND NOT ANYONE LISTENED"

PRETTY SUBTLE, MA'AM..
SCHULZ

I NEED HELP WITH THESE SCIENCE QUESTIONS

"WHY DO WE HAVE FINGERNAILS?"
TO KEEP OUR FINGERS FROM FALLING OFF!

HA HA HA HA HA!

9-14
SCHULZ

BONK!
9-15

HEY, MANAGER.. I'M NOT SURE I WANT TO PLAY RIGHT FIELD ANYMORE..

I WAS STANDING OUT THERE, AND SOMETHING HIT ME ON THE HEAD..

I WONDER WHAT IT COULD HAVE BEEN..
WHO KNOWS? WE LIVE IN A STRANGE WORLD, DON'T WE?

WITH A LOT OF STRANGE PEOPLE..
SCHULZ

RERUN, WHAT'S WRONG?
NOTHING

9-16
NOTHING?

THEN WHY ARE YOU SITTING LIKE THIS?
YOU ARE.. I'M NOT..
SCHULZ

THIS SUPPER DISH IS GETTING PRETTY OLD

MAYBE WE SHOULD GET RID OF IT..

9-17
FOR SALE BY OWNER
SCHULZ

PEANUTS
by SCHULZ
MEMORIES

SIGH

WHY DO I LIVE ALL ALONE OUT HERE IN THE DESERT?

I'M GOING TO TELL YOU SOMETHING I'VE NEVER TOLD ANYONE

YEARS AGO WHEN I WAS YOUNG, I WAS OUT WALKING WITH SOME PEOPLE..
9-18

SUDDENLY, A RABBIT RAN ACROSS IN FRONT OF US!

"GET HIM!" SHOUTED THE PEOPLE!

EVEN THOUGH I DIDN'T WANT TO, I DARTED AFTER THE RABBIT!

I WOULDN'T HAVE KNOWN WHAT TO DO EVEN IF I HAD CAUGHT HIM..

THEN IT HAPPENED! THE RABBIT RAN INTO THE ROAD, AND WAS HIT BY A CAR!

I WAS STUNNED! WHY DID I DO IT?! OH, HOW I HATED MYSELF!

AND HOW I HATED THOSE PEOPLE WHO SHOUTED, "GET HIM!"

SO I CAME OUT HERE TO THE DESERT WHERE I COULDN'T HURT ANYTHING AGAIN

I'VE NEVER TOLD THIS TO ANYONE BEFORE..

I GUESS I STILL HAVEN'T..
SCHULZ

Dear Pen Pal,

WHY DO YOU WANT TO WRITE TO SOMEONE IN ANOTHER COUNTRY YOU DON'T EVEN KNOW?

IT HELPS TO PROMOTE CULTURAL UNDERSTANDING

How are you?
WHEN THEY SEE WRITING LIKE THAT, THEY'LL WANT TO ATTACK US..
9/19
SCHULZ

Dear Pen Pal, School started here last week.
9-20

I won't be able to write as often
I'LL BET HE'LL BE GLAD..
SCHULZ

YES, MA'AM.. I DIDN'T UNDERSTAND THE QUESTION
9-21

NO, MA'AM..OR RATHER, YES, MA'AM..WHO? NO, BEFORE THAT..YES, MA'AM..WHEN? THE QUESTION..WHERE? PROBABLY..WHO? WHERE?
SCHULZ

DON'T SIGH LIKE THAT, MA'AM.. IT BREAKS MY HEART..

MY DAD BOUGHT ME A NEW BALL..
9-22

WELL, LET'S GO TRY IT OUT..

BONK!

SORRY, SIR.. I THOUGHT YOU HAD QUICK HANDS..
SCHULZ

OKAY, MARCIE..I'LL GO DOWN THE FIELD, AND YOU THROW ME THE BALL..

BUT DON'T THROW IT BEFORE I GET DOWN THERE, OR YOU'LL HIT ME ON THE HEAD..

9-23
BONK!

SORRY, SIR.. I WAS PRACTICING MY INTENTIONAL GROUNDING..
SCHULZ

MARCIE, YOU'RE THE MOST NONATHLETIC PERSON IN THE WORLD

WHY WOULD YOUR DAD BUY YOU A FOOTBALL?
9-24

HE SAID, "BECAUSE YOU CAN'T PUNT A VIOLIN!"

HA HA HA HA HA HA!

I THINK YOUR DAD IS MORE WEIRD THAN YOU ARE
SCHULZ

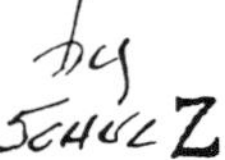
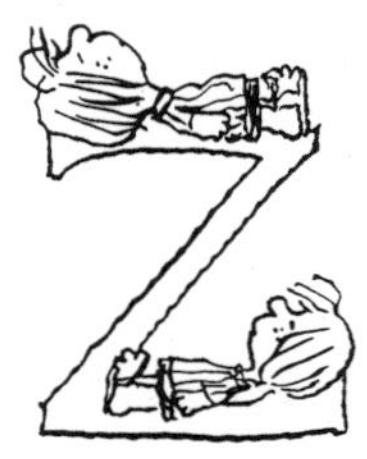
PEANUTS
by SCHULZ

PSST..SIR, DON'T GO TO SLEEP...
Z

Z

I'M AWAKE! GENTLEMEN, START YOUR ENGINES!

SIR, WHY DID YOU SAY, "GENTLEMEN, START YOUR ENGINES!"?
I DIDN'T SAY, "GENTLEMEN, START YOUR ENGINES!"

YES, YOU SAID, "I'M AWAKE! GENTLEMEN, START YOUR ENGINES!"
MARCIE, YOU ARE SO WEIRD!

Z
9-25

GENTLEMEN, START YOUR ENGINES!

I REMEMBER NOW.. IT'S WHAT THEY SAY TO BEGIN THE RACE..
YOU WIN THE WEIRD RACE, MARCIE
PRINCIPAL'S OFFICE
SCHULZ

IT SAYS HERE THAT A BORDER COLLIE CAN HERD 300 SHEEP AT A TIME..
I WONDER HOW THEY DO IT..
FALL IN!
9-26
SCHULZ

A LETTER!

I GOT A LETTER FROM MY PEN PAL IN SCOTLAND!
9-27

"DEAR CHARLIE, JUST BEEN TO THE SHOPS.. MA MAW'S IN BED WITH A SORE HEID AND MA DA'S MAKIN MINCE AND TATTIES FOR THE DINNER..LOVE, MORAG"
SHE DOES PRATTLE ON, DOESN'T SHE?
SCHULZ

Dear Pen Pal
Thank you for writing

I was thrilled to get your letter from Scotland.
ASK HER IF SHE CAN GET ME A STARTING TIME AT ST. ANDREWS..
SCHULZ
9-28

WHY WOULD SOME GIRL IN SCOTLAND WASTE HER TIME WRITING TO YOU?
BECAUSE WE'RE PEN PALS.. MAYBE SHE LIKES MY LETTERS TO HER..
9/29

SOMETIMES PEN PALS FALL IN LOVE..
IT'S A WEE EARLY, LAD, TO BE THINKIN' LIKE THAT..
SCHULZ

Dear Pen Pal,
How is the weather in Glasgow?
ASK HER IF SHE NEEDS A GOOD SHEEP DOG..
9-30

Someday I'd like to go to Scotland.
IF I HAD A SHEEP, I'D HERD IT!
SCHULZ

I LIKE TO OPEN OUR MAILBOX THESE DAYS KNOWING THERE'LL BE A SURPRISE FOR ME FROM SCOTLAND..
10-1

THE LOCH NESS MONSTER!
SCHULZ

PEANUTS
by SCHULZ

ROSEBUD?

HERE, BIG BROTHER..I'VE GOT SOME PAPERS FOR YOU TO SIGN..

WHAT SORT OF PAPERS?
10-2

ON THIS ONE YOU AGREE TO HELP ME WITH MY HOMEWORK EVERY NIGHT FOR THE REST OF YOUR LIFE..

WITH THIS ONE YOU DECLARE THAT ALL THE HELP YOU GIVE ME WILL GUARANTEE PERFECT GRADES..

HERE'S THE THIRD ONE..
THE THIRD ONE?

"I DO EXPLICITLY AFFIRM THAT EVEN THOUGH I SIGNED THE FIRST TWO PAPERS, I AM NOT COMPLETELY OUT OF MY MIND!"
SCHULZ

SOMETIMES I LIE AWAKE AT NIGHT, AND I THINK ABOUT THE GOOD LIFE THAT I HAVE.. I REALLY HAVE NO COMPLAINTS..
10-3

THEN A VOICE COMES TO ME FROM OUT OF THE DARK, "WE APPRECIATE YOUR ATTITUDE!"
SCHULZ

10-4

SLURP!

THROUGH PRACTICING ALREADY?
SCHULZ

Dear Pen Pal,
I haven't heard from you for a while. Are you well?
ASK HER IF SHE NEEDS A SURGEON

Is everything all right?
OR AN ATTORNEY
SCHULZ
10-5

" DEAR CHARLIE, THIS IS YOUR PEN PAL FROM SCOTLAND.."
10-6

" I WOULD HAVE WRITTEN SOONER, BUT I HAVE THIRTY OTHER PEN PALS, AND.."

THIRTY?

I THOUGHT I WAS THE ONLY ONE!
LIFE'S LESSON NUMBER FOUR THOUSAND AND FIFTY..
SCHULZ

I THOUGHT SHE WAS WRITING ONLY TO ME.. THEN SHE TELLS ME SHE HAS THIRTY OTHER PEN PALS!

WELL, LIFE IS LIKE A HELICOPTER, CHARLIE BROWN
LIKE A WHAT?

OR MAYBE A SKATEBOARD.. NO, LIFE IS LIKE A T-SHIRT..
10-7

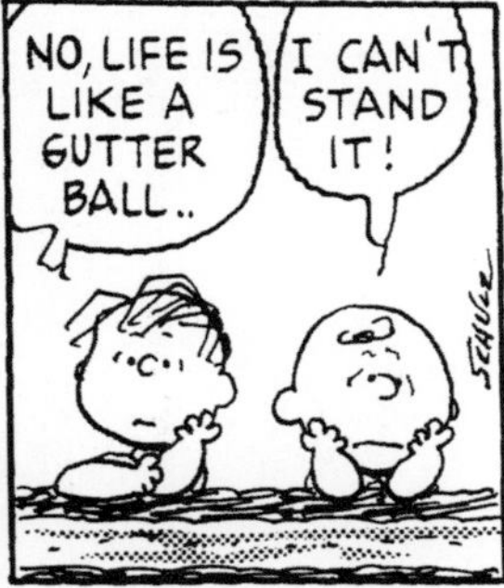
NO, LIFE IS LIKE A GUTTER BALL..
I CAN'T STAND IT!
SCHULZ

MOVE ONE INCH CLOSER, YOU STUPID BEAGLE, AND YOU'LL REGRET IT FOR THE REST OF YOUR LIFE!
10-8

ISN'T IT ODD HOW WE ALL SAY THINGS NOW AND THEN WE DON'T REALLY MEAN?
SCHULZ

PEANUTS
by
SCHULZ

10-9

DO WE HAVE
ANY MARBLES?
SCHULZ

WHY ARE WE PLAYING FOOTBALL IN THE RAIN, SIR?
THIS IS A "DOWN IN THE MUD" GAME, MARCIE
10/10

IT'S SLAM, BANG, ROCK 'EM, SOCK 'EM!

BESIDES THAT, IT'S FUN!!

WHY ARE WE PLAYING FOOTBALL IN THE RAIN, CHARLIE BROWN?
BECAUSE WE'RE OUT OF OUR MINDS!
SCHULZ

I CAN'T PLAY FOOTBALL IN THE RAIN, SIR... MY GLASSES ARE FOGGED UP.. I CAN'T SEE A THING...
10-11

DON'T WORRY ABOUT IT, MARCIE..TACKLE ANYBODY WHO COMES NEAR YOU..

I GOT ONE, SIR!
SCHULZ

10-12
ANOTHER SACK, CHUCK!
ANOTHER MEDIC!
SCHULZ

10-13
TOUCHDOWN!
SOME DOGS GET TO LIE ON A SOFT RUG IN FRONT OF A FIREPLACE AND EAT COOKIES..

10-14
WHO ARE YOU? ARE YOU IN THE FOOTBALL GAME?
WOOF!

AH! NOW I KNOW WHAT YOU ARE..

YOU'RE A DOG, AREN'T YOU? YOU'RE A DOG COVERED WITH MUD!

IT'S BETTER THAN NOTHING

HEY, CHUCK, WE HAD FUN PLAYING FOOTBALL, DIDN'T WE?
10-15

I LOVE THE SLAMMING AND THE BANGING AND SPLASHING THROUGH THE MUD

ADMIT IT, CHUCK, CAN YOU EVER REMEMBER HAVING MORE FUN?

WELL, THERE WAS THE TIME I FELL OUT OF A SWING AND LANDED ON MY HEAD..

PEANUTS
by SCHULZ
RING!

HI!
HI! WHAT'S UP?

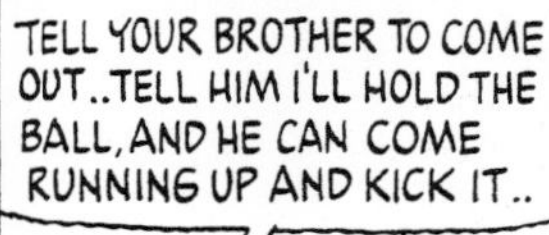
TELL YOUR BROTHER TO COME OUT..TELL HIM I'LL HOLD THE BALL, AND HE CAN COME RUNNING UP AND KICK IT..

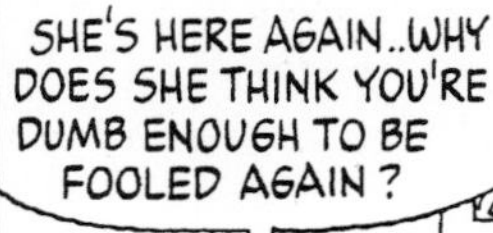
SHE'S HERE AGAIN..WHY DOES SHE THINK YOU'RE DUMB ENOUGH TO BE FOOLED AGAIN?

YOU DON'T REALLY BELIEVE MY BROTHER IS THAT NAÏVE, DO YOU?

I MEAN, AFTER ALL, HOW OFTEN DO YOU THINK YOU CAN FOOL SOMEONE WITH THE SAME TRICK?!

AAUGH!

WUMP!

10-16

PRETTY OFTEN, HUH?

HOW CAN YOU TELL IF A DOG IS INTELLIGENT?
PROBABLY IF HE SEEMS TO BE CURIOUS ABOUT THINGS..
I'VE ALWAYS WONDERED WHAT ANNA KARENINA EVER SAW IN COUNT VRONSKY..
SCHULZ
10-17

Z

Z

SCHULZ
10-18

IF I MOVE, I'LL DISTURB MY DOG..BUT IF I DON'T MOVE, I'LL BE LATE FOR SCHOOL..I NEVER KNOW WHAT TO DO..
10-19

SCHULZ
AND I NEVER KNOW WHAT MY DOG IS THINKING..
THIS IS MY FAVORITE TIME OF DAY..

QUICK, MARCIE.. I NEED YOUR INK ERASER!

10-20

PEEKABOO, MA'AM!
SCHULZ

THAT'S IT? THAT'S THE STORY OF YOUR LIFE?

WELL, THANK YOU FOR SHARING IT WITH US..

10-21
YOU'RE NEXT..
SCHULZ

I CAN'T BELIEVE I'M SITTING HERE IN THE DESERT LISTENING TO A ROCK TELL ME THE STORY OF HIS LIFE..

"HER" LIFE... SORRY..
SCHULZ
10-22

AS THE WORLD FAMOUS HOCKEY COACH, WHAT DO YOU DO WHEN THE OTHER TEAM ATTACKS?

CIRCLE THE ZAMBONIS!

10-23

SCHULZ

10-24
YOU GOT ANOTHER SIX ON THAT HOLE..
I'VE GOT MORE SIXES THAN THE "BOOK OF REVELATION"

WHAT DID YOU PUT DOWN FOR THE THIRD QUESTION, SIR?

"WHERE IS ALBANIA?" I SAID IT'S RIGHT NEXT TO JOE BANIA..
10/25

PRETTY OBVIOUS, HUH, SIR?
VERY OBVIOUS..
SCHULZ

As he turned to leave, he paused, and said,
10-26

"Toodle-oo, Caribou! In a while, Crocodile! Stay loose, Mongoose! It's been neat, Parakeet!"

"Please," she said, "Just leave!"
SCHULZ

SOMETIMES I LIE AWAKE AT NIGHT, AND JUST STARE INTO THE DARKNESS..

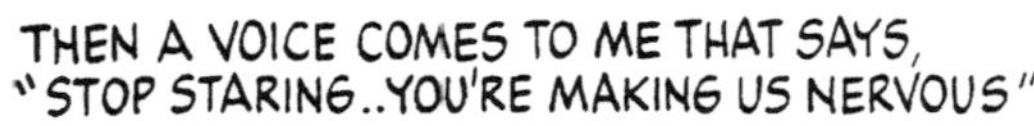
THEN A VOICE COMES TO ME THAT SAYS, "STOP STARING..YOU'RE MAKING US NERVOUS"

10-27

YOU KNOW, OLAF, I THINK WE SHOULD DO MORE THAN JUST EAT AND SLEEP..
10-28

THEY SAY LIFE IS SHORT..
IT IS?

10-29

TURNED COLD LAST NIGHT, DIDN'T IT?

PEANUTS
by SCHULZ

RING!

GOOD MORNING..I'M HERE TO TELL YOU ABOUT THE "GREAT PUMPKIN"
THE WHAT?
10-30

ON HALLOWEEN NIGHT, THE "GREAT PUMPKIN" RISES FROM THE PUMPKIN PATCH, AND BRINGS TOYS TO ALL THE CHILDREN!

WHY SHOULD I BELIEVE THAT?

IT'LL MAKE YOU A BETTER PERSON.. YOU'LL HAVE PEACE AND COMFORT... LOOK AT MY COMPANION HERE..

WAITING FOR THE "GREAT PUMPKIN" HAS BROUGHT HIM PERFECT PEACE..

Z
YES, I CAN SEE THAT..GO AWAY!

I HOPE SHE DIDN'T WAKE YOU UP WHEN SHE SLAMMED THE DOOR..
I WAS DREAMING ABOUT THE "GREAT WHAT'S HIS NAME"
SCHULZ

I LOVE HALLOWEEN.. WITH THESE BINOCULARS WE'LL BE ABLE TO SEE THE "GREAT PUMPKIN" COME FLYING IN!
I CAN SEE THE BIG DIPPER..

I HOPE YOU'RE NOT WASTING YOUR TIME LOOKING AT THE BIG DIPPER..
I CAN SEE THE CRATERS ON THE MOON..
10/31

I HOPE YOU'RE NOT WASTING YOUR TIME LOOKING AT THE MOON..
I CAN SEE A STUPID KID SITTING IN A PUMPKIN PATCH..
SCHULZ

11-1
SO YOU SAT OUT IN A PUMPKIN PATCH ALL NIGHT LOOKING THROUGH SOME BINOCULARS..
I WAS HOPING I COULD SEE THE "GREAT PUMPKIN" COME FLYING IN..
YOU LOOK BETTER THIS WAY.. YOU LOOK LIKE YOU'RE FAR AWAY...
STUPID DOG!
SCHULZ

11-2

OUCH
SCHULZ

FORREST BLIMP!

QUICK, MARCIE.. I NEED THE ANSWER TO THE FIRST QUESTION..

HERE WE GO!

FASTER THAN A FAX, SIR
YOU'RE HUMONGOUSLY WEIRD, MARCIE!

HERE, HOLD THE TEA BAG, PLEASE..

PEANUTS

by
SCHULZ

LAST MONDAY..

SO THIS STRANGE KID SITS OUT IN A PUMPKIN PATCH ALL NIGHT WAITING FOR THE "GREAT PUMPKIN"..

YOU KNOW WHAT I'M THINKING?

WHAT IF THIS "GREAT PUMPKIN" HAD APPEARED IN SCOTLAND, AND THE "LOCH NESS MONSTER" ATE HIM?!

HAHAHAHAHA!

11-6

HAHA
HAHA!

DO DOGS AND BIRDS EVER LAUGH AT PEOPLE?
SCHULZ

WHY AM I STANDING HERE IN THE RAIN WAITING FOR THE SCHOOL BUS?
SO YOU CAN LEARN HOW TO SPELL AND MULTIPLY FRACTIONS
AND LEARN A TRADE, AND MAKE LOTS OF MONEY
SO YOU CAN FEED YOUR DOG
SCHULZ
11-7

DO YOU THINK IT'S POSSIBLE TO FALL IN LOVE ACROSS A CROWDED ROOM?
11/8

PROBABLY

THIS IS A CROWDED ROOM, ISN'T IT?

BUT IT'S NOT AN ENCHANTED EVENING..
RATS!
SCHULZ

YOU HAVE? YOU'VE ACTUALLY FLOWN ABOVE THE CLOUDS?

11-9
WOW! WHAT WAS IT LIKE?

WELL, YOU SHOULDN'T HAVE CLOSED YOUR EYES..
SCHULZ

WINTER IS COMING..

A SHARPNESS IN THE AIR.. SMOKE RISING FROM CHIMNEYS...

THE SOUND OF THE ZAMBONI..
SCHULZ
11-10

I FAILED A BIG TEST TODAY.. ALL THE TRUES WERE FALSE AND ALL THE FALSES WERE TRUE..

THAT'S LIFE.. ALL THE TRUES ARE FALSE AND ALL THE FALSES ARE TRUE

LIFE IS PROBABLY EASIER IF YOU'RE A DOG..
THAT'S TRUE.. OR IS IT FALSE?
11-11

WHAT ARE YOU EATING?
A NEW BREAKFAST CEREAL..

I LIKE THE NAME..

"FLAKEY THINGS"?
11/12
SCHULZ

PEANUTS
by
SCHULZ

Menu

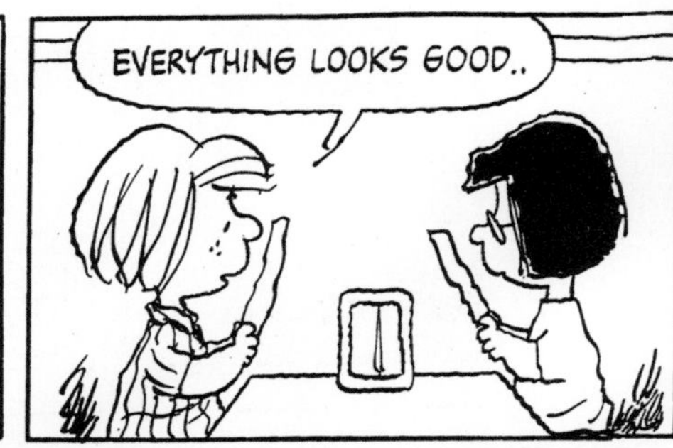
EVERYTHING LOOKS GOOD..

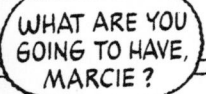

WHAT ARE YOU GOING TO HAVE, MARCIE ?
I DON'T KNOW.. MAYBE JUST A HOT DOG...

I THINK I'LL HAVE A TUNA FISH SANDWICH..

11-13
THAT'S REDUNDANT, SIR

WHAT'S REDUNDANT?
"TUNA FISH" IS REDUNDANT

YOU KNOW, I THINK YOU'RE RIGHT.. THANKS FOR TELLING ME..

I'LL HAVE A FISH SANDWICH !
SCHULZ

11-14
I HEAR YOUR GRAMPA HAS A NEW PHILOSOPHY..
"THE SECRET TO LIFE IS TO BE OLDER THAN YOUR LAWN!"
HOW PROFOUND CAN YOU GET?
SCHULZ

11-15
SCHULZ

I'M YOUR YOUNGER BROTHER, AND I DON'T SUCK MY THUMB OR CLING TO A BLANKET FOR SECURITY..

HOORAY FOR YOU

AS THE YEARS GO BY, YOU'LL PROBABLY DEVELOP A REAL RESENTMENT TOWARD ME..
11-16

AND FIND DIFFERENT WAYS TO GET EVEN..
SCHULZ

HI, MY NAME IS RERUN.. CAN YOUR DOG COME OUT TO PLAY?

WELL, I DON'T KNOW.. I'LL HAVE TO SEE..
11-17

WHO ARE YOU, HIS AGENT?
SCHULZ

I'M SORRY..SNOOPY CAN'T GO OUT TO PLAY RIGHT NOW... HE'S READING..

DOGS CAN'T READ..
11-18

WELL, HE'S SITTING IN THERE HOLDING A BOOK..

THERE'S NO WAY IN THE WORLD THAT ANNA KARENINA AND COUNT VRONSKY COULD EVER HAVE BEEN HAPPY..
SCHULZ

HI, MY NAME IS RERUN.. DO YOU WANT TO COME OUT AND PLAY?

WE'LL HAVE FUN.. I'LL THROW THE BALL, AND YOU CAN CHASE IT...
11-19

SCHULZ
IT WOULD HAVE BEEN FUN!!

PEANUTS
by SCHULZ
NO, IT'S MORE OF A "GOBBLE GOBBLE"

ANYWAY, IT'S FOUR MORE DAYS..

THEY CALL IT "THANKSGIVING"

AND THEY EAT BIRDS! CAN YOU BELIEVE IT?!

WHY WOULD ANYONE WANT TO EAT A BIRD?

11-20
THAT'S GOOD..THEY'LL NEVER BOTHER AN ATTORNEY..
SCHULZ

THIS IS MY REPORT ON THE STORY OF THE FIVE LITTLE HOGS..

OR WAS IT THE SIX LITTLE PIGS?

OR THE NINE LITTLE HOGS, OR SOMETHING LIKE THAT..
11-21

WHICH IS THE KIND OF REPORT YOU GET WHEN YOU WRITE IT WHILE WALKING FROM YOUR DESK TO THE FRONT OF THE ROOM..
SCHULZ

HAVE YOU THOUGHT ABOUT WHAT YOU WANT FOR CHRISTMAS?

A WRISTWATCH? YOU DON'T HAVE ANY WRISTS..
11-22

YOU'D HAVE TO HAVE A WINGWATCH! HA HA HA HA!!

BIRDS HAVE NO SENSE OF HUMOR
SCHULZ

YES, MA'AM? CHARLES DICKENS!
11-23

SIR, HOW DID YOU KNOW THAT?

IF YOU GO TO SCHOOL LONG ENOUGH, SOONER OR LATER THE ANSWER IS GOING TO BE CHARLES DICKENS..
SCHULZ

GET DRESSED..WE'RE ALL GOING OVER TO GRAMMA'S FOR TURKEY

11-24
I DON'T EAT TURKEY ANYMORE.. I'M A VEGETARIAN..

AND WHAT ARE YOU?
I'M A COLD CEREALARIAN!
SCHULZ

BEFORE WE CAN FLY, ALL PILOTS HAVE TO BE EXAMINED BY THE FLIGHT SURGEON..
11-25

HE SAID I CAN FLY.. MY NOSE IS COLD..
SCHULZ

HERE'S THE WORLD WAR I FLYING ACE ZOOMING THROUGH THE AIR ABOVE ENEMY LINES..
11-26

I GOT A LETTER FROM MOM TODAY..SHE ALWAYS WORRIES ABOUT ME..

SHE SAID NOT TO FLY TOO HIGH..
SCHULZ

Admiral Benbow
PEANUTS
by SCHULZ

YES, MA'AM.. RIGHT HERE..

THIS IS MY REPORT ON "TREASURE ISLAND"
11-27

DETAILS RIGHT AFTER LUNCH..

ALL RIGHT, PICKING UP WHERE WE LEFT OFF, THIS IS MY REPORT ON "TREASURE ISLAND."

DETAILS AT ELEVEN..

WELL, WHAT TIME DO YOU GO TO BED, MA'AM?
SCHULZ

MORE ROOT BEER, MONSIEUR FLYING ACE?

HEY, CHARLES.. YOUR DOG'S HERE IN OUR KITCHEN AGAIN..
11-28

HE SEEMED HUNGRY SO I GAVE HIM SOME FRENCH BREAD..

HOW DO YOU GET THE BREAD IN THE TOASTER?
SCHULZ

HERE'S THE WORLD WAR I FLYING ACE WALKING BACK TO THE AERODROME..
11-29

I SEE THERE'S STILL A LIGHT ON IN THE BARRACKS..

I WONDER WHO THAT IS STANDING IN THE DOORWAY...

PROBABLY ONE OF THE COOKS..
SCHULZ

YOU LOOK TIRED..WAS THERE A LOT OF ACTION ON THE WESTERN FRONT?
I MUST BE OUT OF MY MIND..AFTER THE FIFTH ROOT BEER, I REENLISTED!
SCHULZ
11-30

ASK YOUR DOG IF
HE WANTS TO COME
OUT AND PLAY..

12-1

I DON'T KNOW MY
SOCIAL SECURITY NUMBER
SCHULZ

OKAY, RERUN, BEFORE
WE BEGIN THE GAME,
I'LL READ THE RULES...

I LOVE THE
RULES! YOU
CAN'T PLAY A
GAME UNLESS
YOU KNOW
THE RULES!
12-2

YOU NEED RULES
TO BE FAIR..TO
ENJOY ANY GAME
A PERSON MUST
ALWAYS STRIVE
TO BE FAIR!

GOOD..NOW
THE FIRST
THING WE
DO IS DECIDE
WHO..

I WANT
THE RED!!
SCHULZ

I'M GONNA WIN!
I'M GONNA WIN!

WAIT JUST A
MINUTE! IT'S
MY TURN!

12-3
OKAY, YOUR
TURN..

Z
SCHULZ

PEANUTS
by SCHULZ

WHERE ARE YOU GOING?

SANTA CLAUS IS DOWN AT THE CORNER..I HAVE A FEW QUESTIONS TO ASK HIM..

SO, MR. FANCY CLAUS, REMEMBER ME? MY NAME IS RERUN...

WHAT HAPPENED TO ALL THE THINGS YOU WERE GOING TO BRING ME FOR CHRISTMAS LAST YEAR? KIND OF FORGOT, DIDN'T YOU? HUH?!

I DON'T SUPPOSE YOU'D CARE TO EXPLAIN, WOULD YOU, HUH?!

ROWRR!!
12-4

HOW DID IT GO?
WE REALLY DIDN'T TALK THAT MUCH..HE SEEMED PRETTY BUSY..
SCHULZ

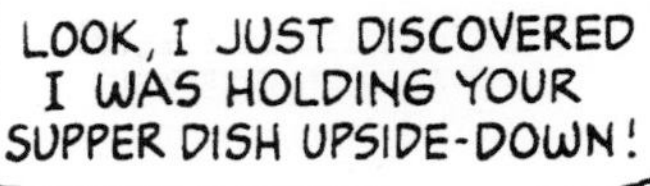

LOOK, I JUST DISCOVERED I WAS HOLDING YOUR SUPPER DISH UPSIDE-DOWN!

12-5

WHAT IF I HADN'T NOTICED IT?

IT'S HARD TO IMAGINE WHAT MIGHT HAVE HAPPENED..LITTLE THINGS LIKE THAT CAN CHANGE YOUR WHOLE LIFE..

MAYBE I'LL JUST GIVE HIM TWO WEEKS' NOTICE..
SCHULZ

I FEEL SORRY FOR THOSE SANTA CLAUSES WHO STAND ON THE SIDEWALK HOUR AFTER HOUR RINGING A BELL..
ME TOO.. I ALWAYS WONDER HOW THEY FEEL AT THE END OF THE DAY..
SCHULZ
12-6

YOU SHOULD WATCH THIS..

THEY'RE SHOWING PICTURES OF HUGE SNOWFLAKES FALLING GENTLY ON THIS BEAUTIFUL SNOW COVERED MEADOW..
12-7

YOU CAN SEE THE SAME THING RIGHT NOW IF YOU GO OUTSIDE..

OUTSIDE?!

SCHULZ

SCHULZ

2-9
"MEN ARE FROM MARS, WOMEN ARE FROM VENUS"

THAT'S A GOOD TITLE.. YOU SHOULD WRITE A BOOK LIKE THAT..

Dogs Are From Jupiter..Cats Are From the Moon
SCHULZ

12-10
YOU'RE NOT TICKLISH, I HOPE..
SCHULZ

PEANUTS
SCHULZ

NO SCHOOL TODAY..
IT'S SNOWING..

12-11
IT'S A REGULAR BLIZZARD.. EVERYTHING IS CLOSED..BUSES AREN'T RUNNING...

POWER LINES ARE DOWN ALL OVER THE CITY.. IT'S THE WORST BLIZZARD SINCE 1806!

HERE'S YOUR LUNCH.. LET'S GO..

MOM SAID YOU COULD HAVE STAYED HOME IN 1806..
I CAN'T SEE WHERE I'M GOING..
SCHULZ

YES, MA'AM, I'D LIKE TO BUY A BOOK OF POEMS FOR THIS GIRL IN MY CLASS..

WELL, SHE'S REALLY OUT OF MY CLASS, BUT WE'RE IN THE SAME CLASS, BUT I'M NOT IN HER CLASS..

12-12

ACTUALLY, SHE PROBABLY DOESN'T KNOW I EVEN EXIST...

DON'T CRY, MA'AM..I'LL SURVIVE..
SCHULZ

PRETTY NEAT, HUH?
12-13

IT'S A BOOK OF ROMANTIC POETRY I BOUGHT FOR A GIRL IN MY CLASS..

IT DIDN'T HAVE A DOG ON THE COVER..
SCHULZ

WHAT'S THIS?
A BOOK OF POETRY..I'M GIVING IT TO A GIRL IN MY CLASS..

WOULDN'T YOU LIKE TO HAVE SOMEONE WHO LOVES YOU GIVE YOU A BOOK OF POETRY?

12-14
I'D RATHER HAVE A TWENTY-DOLLAR GIFT CERTIFICATE..
SCHULZ

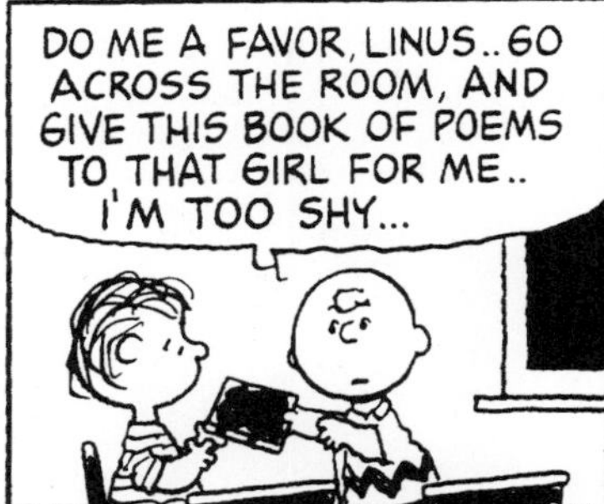
DO ME A FAVOR, LINUS.. GO ACROSS THE ROOM, AND GIVE THIS BOOK OF POEMS TO THAT GIRL FOR ME.. I'M TOO SHY...

WHAT WILL I SAY TO HER?
SAY ANYTHING.. JUST BE SMOOTH...

12-15
HERE, DARLING!
SCHULZ

SORRY, CHARLIE BROWN.. SHE SAYS SHE DOESN'T CARE FOR POETRY.. SHE SAYS SHE DOESN'T EVEN LIKE TO READ

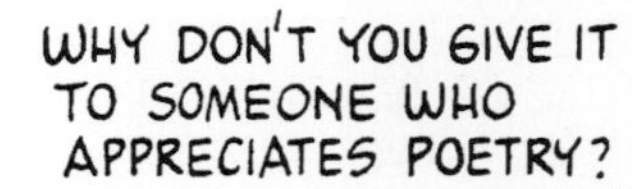
WHY DON'T YOU GIVE IT TO SOMEONE WHO APPRECIATES POETRY?

" IN A FIELD BY THE RIVER MY LOVE AND I DID STAND "
SCHULZ
12-16

YES, MA'AM.. REMEMBER ME?

I WAS IN HERE A FEW DAYS AGO AND BOUGHT A BOOK OF POEMS FOR A GIRL IN MY CLASS..

12-17

SHE DIDN'T LIKE IT... CAN YOU THINK OF ANYTHING ELSE I MIGHT BUY FOR HER?

SOMETHING THAT WOULD REALLY IMPRESS HER, AND MAKE HER LIKE ME MORE THAN ANYONE SHE'S EVER KNOWN..

FOR ABOUT A DOLLAR?
SCHULZ

"AND THE FROG TURNED INTO A PRINCE, AND THEY LIVED HAPPILY EVER AFTER"

Dear Monsieur Claus,

"MONSIEUR" CLAUS?

I SUPPOSE IT NEVER OCCURRED TO YOU THAT HE MIGHT BE FRENCH..
12/19
SCHULZ

12-20

SCHULZ

I THOUGHT IT MIGHT BE NICE TO DROP A LITTLE NOTE TO SANTA CLAUS'S WIFE..

Dear Signora Claus,

"SIGNORA"?
I HAVE A THEORY THAT HE MARRIED A NICE ITALIAN GIRL..
SCHULZ
12-21

YOU BUILT A GREAT SNOWMAN..
THANK YOU..

STAND CLOSER..HE WANTS TO SHAKE HANDS..
12-22
SCHULZ

RATS! NO ONE SENT ME A CHRISTMAS CARD..

WELL, DID YOU SEND ANY YOURSELF?
DID I WHAT?

DID YOU SEND ANY YOURSELF?

DID I WHAT?
SCHULZ
12-23

SOMEDAY, I'M GOING TO LIVE IN A BIG HOUSE WITH A FIREPLACE, AND ON CHRISTMAS EVE I'LL HANG MY STOCKING ON THE FIREPLACE, AND SANTA CLAUS WILL COME AND FILL MY STOCKING WITH WONDERFUL PRESENTS...
IN THE MEANTIME, MY ARM IS FALLING OFF!
12-24
SCHULZ

PEANUTS
by SCHULZ

HERE, I GUESS THIS IS FOR YOU..

A CHRISTMAS PRESENT FROM WOODSTOCK! WOW!

THIS IS EXCITING! I WONDER WHAT IT IS...

BIRDSEED?!
12-25

WHAT AM I GOING TO DO WITH A PACKAGE OF BIRDSEED?

WHY GIVE SOMEBODY SOMETHING THEY CAN'T USE?

SCHULZ

CHRISTMAS "THANK YOU" LETTERS ARE IMPORTANT.. THEY SHOULD ALWAYS BE WRITTEN PROMPTLY...

Dear Grandma, Thank you for the pretty doll you sent me. Too bad it fell in the river.

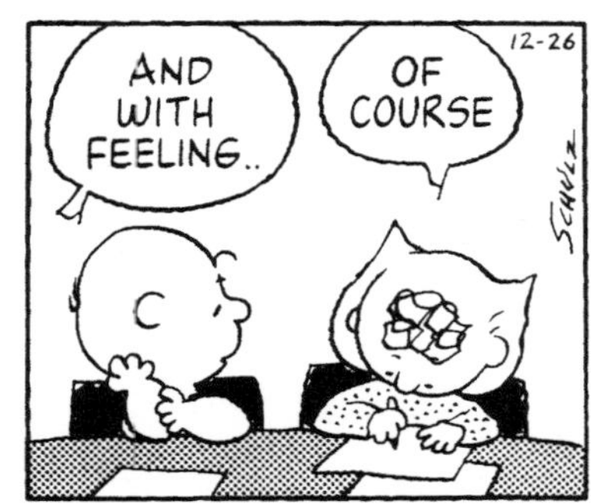
12-26
AND WITH FEELING..
OF COURSE
SCHULZ

IF YOU'RE A TUMBLEWEED, LET'S SEE YOU TUMBLE..
12-27

CAN YOU DO A BACK FLIP?

COULD YOU DO IT ON ICE SKATES?
SCHULZ

I DON'T KNOW WHY, BUT I THOUGHT I MIGHT GET A LOVE LETTER TODAY..

SOMETIMES A LOVE LETTER WILL GET DROPPED IN THE SNOW, AND YOU DON'T FIND IT UNTIL SPRING..

THE SAME THING HAPPENS WITH A HOCKEY PUCK..
SCHULZ
12-28

I THINK THERE'S SOMETHING YOU SHOULD KNOW..
WHAT'S THAT ?

THE WORLD DOES NOT REVOLVE AROUND YOU !

12-29

YOU'RE KIDDING !
SCHULZ

SO HERE I AM ALL ALONE IN THE CAR WHILE THE FAMILY GOES SHOPPING..
12-30

I USED TO GET LONELY, BUT NOT ANYMORE..

SCHULZ

I SEE THE BIRDS ARE ALL PREPARED FOR WINTER..
12-31
SCHULZ

THE WORLD IS FILLED WITH MONDAYS..

1922 **CHARLES M. SCHULZ** 2000

CHARLES M. SCHULZ WAS BORN NOVEMBER 26, 1922, in Minneapolis. His destiny was foreshadowed when an uncle gave him, at the age of two days, the nickname "Sparky" (after the racehorse Spark Plug in the newspaper strip *Barney Google*).

Schulz grew up in St. Paul. By all accounts, he led an unremarkable, albeit sheltered, childhood. He was an only child, close to both parents, his eventual career path nurtured by his father, who bought four Sunday papers every week — just for the comics.

An outstanding student, he skipped two grades early on, but began to flounder in high school — perhaps not so coincidentally at the same time kids are going through their cruelest, most status-conscious period of socialization. The pain, bitterness, insecurity, and failures chronicled in *Peanuts* appear to have originated from this period of Schulz's life.

Although Schulz enjoyed sports, he also found refuge in solitary activities: reading, drawing, and watching movies. He bought comic books and Big Little Books, pored over the newspaper strips, and copied his favorites — *Buck Rogers*, the Walt Disney characters, *Popeye*, *Tim Tyler's Luck*. He quickly became a connoisseur; his heroes were Milton Caniff, Roy Crane, Hal Foster, and Alex Raymond.

In his senior year in high school, his mother noticed an ad in a local newspaper for a correspondence school, Federal Schools (later called Art Instruction Schools). Schulz passed the talent test, completed the course, and began trying, unsuccessfully, to sell gag cartoons to magazines. (His first published drawing was of his dog, Spike, and appeared in a 1937 *Ripley's Believe It or Not!* installment.)

After World War II had ended and Schulz was discharged from the army, he started submitting gag cartoons to the various magazines of the time; his first breakthrough, however, came when an editor at *Timeless Topix* hired him to letter adventure comics. Soon after that, he was hired by his alma mater, Art Instruction, to correct student lessons returned by mail.

Between 1948 and 1950, he succeeded in selling seventeen cartoons to the *Saturday Evening Post* — as well as, to the local *St. Paul Pioneer Press*, a weekly comic feature called *Li'l Folks*. It was run in the women's section and paid ten dollars a week. After writing and drawing the feature for two years, Schulz asked for a better location in the paper or for daily exposure, as well as a raise. When he was turned down on all three counts, he quit.

He started submitting strips to the newspaper syndicates. In the spring of 1950, he received a letter from the United Feature Syndicate, announcing its interest in his submission, *Li'l Folks*. Schulz boarded a train in June for New York City; more interested in doing a strip than a panel, he also brought along the first installments of what would become *Peanuts* — and that was what sold. (The title, which Schulz loathed to his dying day, was imposed by the syndicate.) The first *Peanuts* daily appeared October 2, 1950; the first Sunday, January 6, 1952.

Prior to *Peanuts*, the province of the comics page had been that of gags, social and political observation, domestic comedy, soap opera, and various adventure genres. Although *Peanuts* changed, or evolved, during the fifty years Schulz wrote and drew it, it remained, as it began, an anomaly on the comics page — a comic strip about the interior crises of the cartoonist himself. After a painful divorce in 1973 from which he had not yet recovered, Schulz told a reporter, "Strangely, I've drawn better cartoons in the last six months

— or as good as I've ever drawn. I don't know how the human mind works." Surely, it was this kind of humility in the face of profoundly irreducible human question that makes *Peanuts* as universally moving as it is.

Diagnosed with cancer, Schulz retired from *Peanuts* at the end of 1999. He died on February 12, 2000, the day before his last strip was published (and two days before Valentine's Day) — having completed 17,897 daily and Sunday strips, each and every one fully written, drawn, and lettered entirely by his own hand — an unmatched achievement in comics.

— GARY GROTH

Charles M. Schulz in his home studio at the drawing board, Santa Rosa, California, mid-1990s: courtesy of the Charles M. Schulz Museum.